THIRTY
BY 30

HOW TO PLAN THE PERFECT WEDDING

HANNAH B. FRANKLIN

ISBN 978-1-64468-398-9 (Paperback)
ISBN 978-1-64468-399-6 (Digital)

Covenant Books, Inc.
11661 Hwy 707
Murrells Inlet, SC 29576
www.covenantbooks.com

CONTENTS

INTRODUCTION

Most girls dream of their perfect wedding day from a very young age. They dream of prince charming sweeping them off their feet and living a "happily ever after" life. When I was growing up, I had friends who said, "I better be married by the time I am twenty and having children by the time I am twenty-five years old." I had friends who researched and looked for engagement rings since high school. I, on the other hand, never thought much about my wedding day. I guess I figured I would get married one day, but it was never a big deal for me. I have never wanted children, so while, yes, I think I would like to get married one day, I have found contentment in being single for now and waiting for the perfect guy to come along.

I grew up in a tiny town in rural Pennsylvania where everyone knew everyone and had a graduating class around one hundred and eighty people. After high school, I wanted to move to a city and experience the world. While I was in college at Towson University, I was in a Christian organization that became very much like a "Christian dating circuit," kind of like Grey's Anatomy but without all the sex. Many guys and girls quickly paired and dated each other which would result in some awkward situations as we were all in the same small circle of friends. Well, anyway, with this close circle of friends, many people very quickly got engaged and married soon after graduation. I hung out with friends who were a year older than me, so I started getting invited to weddings while I was still in college.

Before college, I had never been to a wedding, then within eight years, I had been invited to more than thirty different weddings. As I started getting invited to more and more weddings, I began to make a game out of it. It became a big joke with all of my close friends. I set an arbitrary goal to be invited to thirty weddings by the time I was 30 years old. While there were a few of the weddings I was unable to attend, I can honestly say I have been invited to thirty-three weddings, attended twenty-eight, was in three, handed out programs in two, planned one, traveled to Saudi Arabia for one, and crashed one in Egypt. Not to mention the countless beach weddings I have seen on vacation, as well as the weddings I have planned as an event manager.

After completing graduate school, I did a career change from elementary special education into the hospitality industry. I have had the opportunity to see weddings and events from behind the scenes. I have worked countless weddings on both the planning and operations teams, ensuring that the day of the wedding runs flawlessly. I have seen the good, the bad, and the ugly when it comes to weddings and believe that I have seen enough to know the ins and outs of how to plan the perfect wedding. In the following pages, I will share what I believe to be the best tips on how to plan the perfect wedding to ensure you and your guests have a great time, and some of the fun stories from all the weddings I have attended. You can't forget the weddings where the father of the bride forgot his pants or the best man forgot the rings. Or what about the bridezilla who was so demanding she lost a friend through the wedding planning process.

As I share all this information, I do want you to remember that your wedding is just one day of your life. It is the beginning of a new chapter in your life. It should be exciting and a memorable day; an experience you will never forget, but your marriage is what is most important. I urge you to spend your engagement continuing to fall in love with your fiancé and work on the relationship. Remember that the wedding day is just one day—the first day of your forever marriage with your new spouse. I hope that you are marrying your best friend, and your marriage will bring a lifetime of love and happiness!

Now, let's get planning!

The Wedding from Hell

Needless to say, it was not a very enjoyable rehearsal dinner. Shannon was certainly not happy, and we all knew. She threw a tantrum in the middle of the restaurant, yelling at Steve about wanting to kick people out. Her voice got louder and louder, and eventually, everyone in the restaurant could hear, and it was really awkward.

Have you experienced one of those weddings where nothing went as planned or dealt with that crazy bride that was so demanding she lost all her friends? I am sure most of us have, at least, heard those stories if not had firsthand experience with this type of wedding. My friend, Shannon, was so excited to get married, but from the very beginning, I knew we were going to run into issues.

If you know anyone with a type *A* personality, you know that they have to have everything their way, and it has to be perfect. All she wanted all her life was to get married and be a mommy. She had found what seemed to be the perfect guy for her. It really was a crazy story of how they met, but soon after dating, they both just knew, they wanted to spend the rest of their lives together. He proposed, and the wedding planning quickly began.

Shannon had a number of friends from childhood through college that she wanted to be a part of her special day. She asked eight of her closest girlfriends to be her bridesmaids. All the girls were excited to be able to be a part of Shannon's special day. As time passed, Shannon did a lot of the planning and preparation for the big day. She made the invitations, centerpieces, and many other items for the wedding. She tried to include her bridesmaids with as much stuff as possible, but because we all lived miles apart—some in different states—it made it difficult.

Shannon picked a date to go wedding dress shopping and invited many of the girls. As you can imagine, emotions can run high when trying to pick out the perfect wedding dress and stay within a reasonable budget. Shannon had narrowed it down and was deciding between two different dresses. She liked them both and could not decide which one was best. Shannon had wished she could see both dresses on at the same time. We all took pictures of her in both dresses, but in her mind, that was not good enough.

Then, the sales associate had what she thought was a great suggestion. "Why don't you have one of your bridesmaids try on one dress and you try on the other so you can see them side by side?"

All the bridesmaids looked at each other and whispered, "I don't want to try on a wedding dress!"

No one wanted to hurt Shannon's feelings, but we were not there to try on dresses; we were there to offer support to Shannon. Bridesmaid Ester was the closest to Shannon's size, so she became the lucky one and reluctantly tried on the dress.

This was a terrible idea! Ester was not married and had never tried on wedding dresses before. Most girls dream about picking out their wedding dress, and it was completely inappropriate for the sales associate to suggest someone else try on the dress. Ester was a bit upset because she did not want to try on the wedding dress, but of course, she did not want to make Shannon upset, so she did it for the bride.

Fast-forward a few weeks, and now, it is time to pick out the bridesmaid's dresses. The bride and some of her girls headed back to the bridal shop for a "fun-filled" day of dress shopping. Now, Shannon had already had in her mind what dress she wanted us all to wear; we were just there to try them on and order them.

Oh my gosh, this was a disaster. I had never felt so uncomfortable in a dress in my life! Even the sales associate told me, "You look terrible in that dress!"

Now, when the sales associate tells you that you look bad, you know you look bad. I talked to Shannon and tried to convince her to let us try on other dresses. She was very reluctant and started to get upset because she had this dress picked out and was set on it.

I told her, "Shannon, this is your wedding, I will wear what you want me to wear, but I look terrible and uncomfortable in this dress. Can we please at least try on some other options?"

Shannon was still a little reluctant since she was set on that one particular dress, but after our conversation, she was a little more open to other ideas. We each got to pick out two to three dresses we liked, and we found a dress that looked much better on all of us.

For all those ladies who have been in a wedding, you know that bridesmaid dress shopping is never as much fun as they portray it in the movies. And I don't know about you, but in all the weddings I have been to, I have only been to one wedding where I felt all the bridesmaids looked great in their dress. It is hard to put different body shapes and sizes all in the same dress and expect everyone to look good.

Next came the bridal shower and bachelorette party. Over the years, bridal showers and bachelorette parties have become this huge to-do and no longer just an intimate small party for the bride. Typically, the bridesmaids are expected to shell out hundreds of dollars to put together an unforgettable shower and then plan a weekend getaway for the bachelorette party. The wedding industry is beginning to get a bit out of control, and brides have taken things a little too far with the expectations for their bridesmaids.

Back to Shannon's bridal shower, all the bridesmaids had a task, and knowing how Shannon is, we wanted this shower to be perfect. The shower was lovely, and many of Shannon's friends and family members came. She was very happy and thankful to have such great people in her life.

Unfortunately, Shannon definitely treated some of her bridesmaids different than the rest. One of the bridesmaids who had worked hard to help put the shower together was feeling disrespected and started to get frustrated. Shannon kept putting unrealistic expectations on the bridesmaids for what she wanted us to do, and Evelyn just could not take it anymore. At the end of the bridal shower, Shannon and Evelyn got into a huge fight, and Evelyn quit the wedding. She felt as though Shannon was not treating her right and did not want to be a part of her wedding anymore.

Now, Shannon and Evelyn had been friends for years, and their families were good friends, but Evelyn had had enough, and she and her family all decided not to attend Shannon's wedding. The girls are still not friends to this day. Weddings are supposed to be a celebration and a happy time for all involved, but unfortunately, weddings can bring out the worst in people, and this wedding was certainly doing that.

After the whole fiasco with Evelyn quitting the wedding, Shannon tried to be a little more aware of her expectations for her bridesmaids, but she really did not feel like she did anything wrong. The remaining seven bridesmaids helped Shannon as much as we could to get the final touches for the wedding done before the big day, but we were all a little tired of Shannon's attitude and just wanted the wedding to be over.

Shannon's mom tried to help as well, but Shannon and her mom did not always agree on how things should be done. Shannon's mom tends to do whatever she wants and does not really care about the repercussions. If she had an idea or wanted something to be one way, she would just do it without talking to Shannon. The way Shannon's mom acted caused a lot of tension between Shannon and her mom the weeks leading up to the wedding.

* * * * *

The wedding weekend had finally arrived. Shannon had planned a special outing for the entire bridal party a day before the rehearsal. Most of the bridal party had to travel to attend the wedding, so she tried to make it a fun trip for those in the wedding and not just come for the big day. We all piled into our cars and drove about an hour away to go on a surprise adventure. No one knew where we were going except for Shannon and her fiancé, Steve. We ended up at a beautiful winery, and we went hot-air-ballooning! It was a gorgeous morning, and we were all so excited!

We were divided up and assigned a balloon to hop in. None of us had ever been hot-air-ballooning before, and we were all so excited. Our group was divided into three different balloons, and there were a few other balloons that took off around the same time we did. We all floated around for about an hour before it was time to start heading back to reality. Then, all of a sudden, we saw one balloon floating really low and getting closer and closer to the electrical wires.

As we notice this, we informed the balloon director in our basket, "Sir, sir, excuse me, but I am pretty sure that balloon is going to hit the electrical wires."

"Just relax, I am sure they see the wires, and they will not run into them. We do this all the time," replied the balloon director.

Then, as they get closer, we all start screaming, "Stop! stop! Look where you are going, you are going to hit the electrical wires. stop!"

We all screamed as we realized they do not see the wires and were about to run right into it. The next thing we knew, the balloon hit the electrical wires, caught on fire, and the basket dropped to the ground. We were all terrified!

We did not know if anyone in that basket was hurt or if anyone was part of our group. We all panicked, but there was nothing we could do. It was one of the most terrifying things in the world.

Luckily, no one was seriously injured, just a few bumps and bruises and, of course, very shaken up. Also, no one from our group was in that basket. Well, needless to say, that quickly brought our fun to a halt, and we just wanted to get out of the hot-air balloon as soon as possible and walk on solid ground.

This was certainly not quite the adventure Shannon and Steve were hoping for when they were planning this trip. Looking back on this now, this was just the beginning of fiasco after fiasco that happened that wedding weekend.

* * * * *

Next item on the agenda for the wedding weekend was the rehearsal and rehearsal dinner. Not everyone in the wedding party could attend the rehearsal. I can understand emergencies come up, but if you can't even make the rehearsal, then, you might want to reconsider being a bridesmaid. Attending the rehearsal and all the wedding weekend festivities is kind of a big deal if you are in the wedding. I was the only bridesmaid that attended all the events leading up to the wedding.

The rehearsal went just as planned, but the rehearsal dinner, on the other hand, was not ideal. Shannon and Steve wanted to invite many of their out-of-town family and friends, as well as everyone in the wedding to the dinner, but picked a location that was way too small for so many people. Some people invited others and there were not enough seats in the restaurant to accommodate everyone that showed up. The restaurant staff gathered chairs from the back and squeezed people into the tables. Everyone started eating, but since more people showed up than expected, there was not enough food. Now, there are people feeling squished at the tables, hungry, and the restaurant was starting to get really hot. This was one of the hottest days of the year, and the restaurant's air conditioning could not keep up with so many people in such a small place.

Needless to say, it was not a very enjoyable rehearsal dinner. Shannon was certainly not happy, and we all knew. She threw a tantrum in the middle of the restaurant, yelling at Steve about wanting to kick people out. Her voice got louder and louder, and eventually, everyone in the restaurant could hear, and it was really awkward. No one knew what to do, so everyone quickly tried to eat their dinner and get out of there as soon as possible. Some people even just stopped eating and left right away. The wedding weekend was clearly not off to a good start.

After surviving the rehearsal dinner, most of the bridesmaids headed to Shannon's house to spend the night and get ready for the wedding the next morning. Morning came, and the big day had finally arrived. Shannon was so excited, but at this point, we were all just ready to get this day over. Shannon continued to be her demanding self and had a minute-by-minute timeline of the day's events.

While I love a good schedule as much as the next person, this schedule was so detailed and a bit unrealistic. There are going to be things that go wrong throughout the day, and Shannon did not account for that. She expected everything to be absolutely perfect, and we all had to fall in line with her expectations.

We all got dressed and headed to the hair salon to get our hair done for the day, but when we arrived, the salon was closed. After a few frantic phone calls, we found out that the hairdresser never wrote the appointment down in the books and was out of town for the day. Let me tell you; this threw Shannon into a tailspin. Already, things were not looking good. We called around and finally found a salon that could squeeze us in, but of course, we had to pay a premium, and Shannon expected each of us to pay.

Time was running out and not everyone would be able to get their hair professionally done. This was absolutely not the way to start things off. With everyone but one bridesmaid's hair finished, we left the salon and headed back to Shannon's house to get dressed. We are now running late. One girl still has to do her hair, and no one had done their makeup yet. This was a recipe for disaster. Shannon was in tears and getting madder by the minute.

There was nothing we can do to help console her. We all rushed around, finished getting ready, and put our dresses on. We helped Shannon get her wedding dress on and dry her tearing eyes. The photographer was there, and we did not want her to get pictures of the tantrum.

After all the drama in the morning, we finally arrived at the church. At this point, we just needed to get through the ceremony and get Shannon married. We were hoping no other fiascos would happen, and Shannon can enjoy the rest of the day. It was a scorching hot day, and of course, the limo that we took to the church had a broken air conditioning. While it was only a ten-minute drive from Shannon's house to the church, it felt like an hour. By the time we got there, we were all a sweaty mess, and all of our hair and makeup were ruined. I could not believe it. It was almost so terrible the only thing you could do was laugh. Of course, Shannon was not laughing.

The wedding ceremony finally began. The groom and the officiant were upfront, and the groomsmen and bridesmaids started walking down the aisle. Mind you, the groom had no idea of what kind of hell the bride had gone through that morning and the tantrums she had thrown because it had not gone perfectly.

The wedding went on for what seemed to be hours. The church did not have central air conditioning, just some window fans, and we were all extremely hot. At one point, one of the bridesmaids had to sit down because she thought she was going to pass out. We were nearing the end of the ceremony, and the officiant asked the best man for the rings. The look on the best man's face was priceless. He suddenly realized he did not have the rings. Everyone, at first, thought he was just joking, but he was mortified. He had forgotten the rings in the car. He jumped off the stage and ran to the parking lot. Little did he know that he would get locked out of the church and have to run around to a door on the other end of the building. It literally took like fifteen minutes for him to go get the rings. Talk about an awkward few minutes.

We made it through the rest of the ceremony, and now, it was time for the bridal party to take pictures. The wedding guests were then on their own for the next two hours before the cocktail hour and reception was to begin. The entire bridal party and family stuck around to take pictures and then hopped in the limo, still really hot, to take some pictures outside. After all the pictures were over, we headed back to Shannon's house to get our cars to drive to the reception. Unfortunately, the house was locked, and no one had a key. Things were just not going our way. A couple of the groomsmen broke into one of the windows and got us into the house, but now, we were really late for the reception.

Luckily, all the guests from the wedding could enjoy some food and cocktails as they waited for us since we were so late. Except there were no escort cards for the tables, so no one knew where they were supposed to sit. People started taking their seats, and then, they were told they had to get up and move. The wedding coordinator at the venue forgot to set out the escort cards before the reception started, and everyone just entered the room and took a seat. I was told it was a hot mess. The bride did not find out about this until after the wedding; thank goodness!

I don't remember the food, but I don't remember most wedding food. The evening was moving along and then came the slideshow. I don't know about you, but I am not a fan of wedding slideshows. Sorry to all my friends who had them at their weddings; it is not necessary. If you are going to do a slideshow, have it off in the background on loop for people to enjoy on their own time. Do *not* make people sit and watch a twenty-minute slideshow of pictures from when you were a baby until now. With social media these days, all your friends and family have most likely seen all the pictures anyway. Save the time and money and skip the slideshow. Your guests will thank you. Okay, I will get off my soapbox now.

By the time it was time for dancing, there was only thirty minutes left of the reception. For me, the DJ and dancing make or break the wedding. Weddings that don't have a lot of dancing are not as memorable for me. At this particular wedding, after all the formal dances, slideshow, and special requests the bride and groom wanted, the DJ was finally ready to get the party started.

Everyone ran out to the dance floor except for the bride. She started throwing another tantrum because the DJ did something out of order, and it was not the time for everyone to get up and dance. Instead of going with the flow and dancing with all her friends, Shannon was in the corner throwing a fit. Some of the bridesmaids and Shannon's mother were trying to console her, but at this point, so much had gone wrong throughout the day there was nothing you could say or do to make it better.

This was one wedding from hell that I hope never to experience again. While there will obviously be things that might go wrong on your wedding day, the way you handle it makes a big difference. The rest of this book will talk about my experience with all the weddings I have been to and how to plan well, so you do not encounter all the terrible things that happened at this wedding. After each chapter there is a section for you to take notes to help you as you plan your perfect wedding.

Getting Ready

The bride thought she had picked out the perfect dress she wanted us all to wear. When I put on the dress, she had picked out, oh my gosh, it looked terrible! I had never felt so uncomfortable in a dress before. Even the sales associate told me, "Girl, you do not look good in that dress." You know you don't look good when the sales associate tells you that.

Being a Bridesmaid

Today is the big day; the day you have dreamt of for years. It is your wedding day. You have spent months planning and preparing, and it all comes down to this one day. Are you ready to have the best day of your life? Your wedding will be a day you will remember forever.

In most of the weddings I have been to, the bride has her best girlfriends surrounding her as bridesmaids. Being a bridesmaid or maid of honor is no easy task. You are supposed to be the bride's biggest supporter throughout the whole engagement and wedding process. You need to be there for the bride through the stressful planning process and emotional roller coaster the bride will go through leading up to the wedding. Not to mention, the bridal showers, bachelorette party, and of course, the wedding. Being a bridesmaid is a big responsibility, and no one should take it lightly.

Being in a friend's wedding should be an honor, not a dread. If you are not excited to be a part of a friend's wedding, then don't say yes. To enjoy the experience and truly be there for the bride, you have to want to do it, and there is nothing wrong with saying no. As the bride, you should choose wisely of who you want to support you and stand by you on your wedding day.

Unfortunately, due to the high level of stress, weddings can bring out the worst in people, and the last thing you want to do is lose a friend through the wedding process. I have heard horror stories of bridezillas and brides losing friends. I recently had a friend "quit" a wedding. She was supposed to be the maid of honor, but due to the lack of respect and unreasonable expectations the bride had for her, she decided the stress and disrespect from her friend were not worth it. She merely quit being the maid of honor and will not attend the wedding.

In this particular case, Kasey, the maid of honor who quit the wedding, was not that close to the bride, Susan. These two girls were close when they were in high school, and their families were good friends, but over the years, they had drifted apart. When it came time for Susan to get married, she asked her friend to be the maid of honor. Kasey was a bit taken aback as they were not that close anymore and asked Susan why her.

Susan told Kasey, "I know you will do an excellent job as my maid of honor because you have done it before."

I don't know about you but choosing a maid of honor that you have not talked to in a few years simply because they have done it before does not seem like a recipe for success to me. Selecting your maid of honor and bridesmaids should be done carefully and with thoughtful consideration. You want to handpick girls that you are close with and are going to support you through this exciting yet stressful time of your life.

Never feel obligated to ask a friend to be in your wedding just because you were in her wedding. If you are no longer close with that friend or you have other friends who are closer that you want to stand beside you as bridesmaids, then, don't feel like you have to ask this friend out of obligation. "Weddings are no time for quid pro quo. You don't need to ask someone to be in your wedding because they asked you to be in their wedding. Don't ask the college roommate you haven't spoken to in five years just to return the favor" (Zaleski 2017). You are not obligated to ask anyone to be a bridesmaid. It is an honor and a privilege, and as the bride, you get to decide who you want to stand beside you.

One of the worst things about being a bridesmaid is the cost. Being in a wedding is expensive. "After adding up the cost of the dress, accessories, travel expenses, wedding gifts, and more, WeddingChannel.com found that it costs about $1,695 to be a bridesmaid" (Steinberg 2011). As a bride, when doing the planning and picking out what your bridesmaids are going to wear, it is imperative to keep the cost and how much you are expecting each bridesmaid to spend in mind. While your friends should be excited to be in your wedding, they do not want to spend their life savings on your wedding.

Timeline

For many brides, the second they get engaged, they immediately jump into planning mode. They get so excited by the idea of a wedding and getting married, their brain starts racing on everything that needs to get done, and they go full force ahead into full planning mode. While it is essential to get a jump start on planning, and if you have a particular date or location in mind, you will need to book it early, but take some time to celebrate and enjoy being engaged before getting bogged down with all the wedding planning details. A bride should be more excited about the marriage than just the wedding day.

One mistake many brides make is getting ahead of themselves in the planning process and asking too many friends or not the right friends to be in their wedding. Not everyone can be in the wedding, and the girls you choose to stand beside you really matters, so take time to really think through who you want standing beside you on your big day. Be prepared that some girls might get their feelings hurt if you do not ask them to be in your wedding or if they are not your maid of honor. Don't let this get to you. Your wedding is your day, and you get to choose who is in the wedding. You cannot pick everyone, and if their feelings are that hurt, and they are not just excited for you, then, maybe, they are not that good of a friend anyway. There is no right or wrong person to choose, but I would certainly advise picking friends that you are very close with and you know that will support you no matter what.

Depending on how long your engagement is will help determine how early to ask your friends to be in the wedding. If you are planning on having longer-than-a-year engagement, then, you should certainly wait to ask your friends to be in the wedding. "The best rule is to ask your friends, and family members, to be your bridesmaids anywhere between a year to eight months before your wedding. That will give them enough time to plan the bachelorette party and get their dresses. Any less time may not be enough for them to be able to make the commitment" (Glantz 2017). Any earlier than that and you run the risk of having people in your wedding that in a year from now, you are not that close to anymore.

When it comes to wedding dress and bridesmaid dress shopping, you don't want to get these too early. While some women have their dress picked out even before getting engaged, I would advise selecting the date, venue, and colors before purchasing any dresses. You might have something in mind, but until you know exactly when and where you are getting married, your idea of what your wedding gown will look like will most likely change based on the time of year and location of the ceremony and reception. Your colors will also help in selecting any type of pop of color or "extra" item you may add to your gown. I would also advise purchasing your bridal gown before the bridesmaid dresses. You want your bridesmaid's dresses to coordinate well with your dress, not the other way around.

Once again, there is no need to purchase your wedding gown or the bridesmaid dresses more than a year out. I would say you could start bridal gown shopping about nine to twelve months out. You will most likely need to get the dress altered which typically takes a few visits to the bridal shop and may take a few months, so you certainly don't want to wait until the last minute.

Bridesmaid dresses, on the other hand, can be purchased four to six months prior to the wedding. There really is no need to purchase the dress any earlier than that, unless the particular dress you want your bridesmaids to wear is a limited addition or no longer being manufactured. A lot can happen in a year, if you order your bridesmaids dresses too early you run the risk of bridesmaids gaining/losing weight or married bridesmaids being pregnant and the dress no longer fitting. Your bridesmaid dresses might need to be altered but does not take nearly as much time as a bridal gown and can be taken to a local seamstress and be done in a week or two.

Booking hair and makeup appointments should be done four to six months in advance as well. Salons book up fast, and for a large wedding party, you will want to make sure to make your appointments early.

The *Dress*

A close second of the worst thing about being a bridesmaid is the dress. I don't know about you, but it is tough to find a dress that looks flattering on all different body types. I have only been to one wedding where I felt that all the bridesmaids looked great in the dress. While I understand all the attention should be on the bride, I really don't know why bridesmaid's dresses are so ugly. Not to mention, why are they so expensive?

People always say, "Oh, this is perfect, and you will be able to wear it again someday." That is a lie! I have never worn my bridesmaid's dresses again for another occasion. Bridesmaid's dresses look like bridesmaid's dresses, and people can tell, it is not something you will wear again. Unless the bride allows the girls to pick out their dress from a nonbridal shop, you will not wear the dress again.

I have seen weddings that are not as formal, and the bride does not want the bridesmaids to have to purchase expensive dresses that they will only wear once, so they decide on a color, and everyone can wear what they want. Allowing the bridesmaids to wear what they want is an excellent alternative for a budget-conscious wedding. Although, I like when all the bridesmaids are wearing the same dress or at least similar dresses, it does not have to be a dress from a bridal shop. Macy's, Nordstrom, J.Crew, Bloomingdales, and BHLDN (Anthropologie's sister store) all have dynamic bridal departments to find the perfect wedding or bridesmaid dress.

At one of the weddings I was in, the bride wanted the bridesmaids to wear different style dresses but wanted to make sure all the bridesmaids felt comfortable in their dresses. There were two separate styles of dresses to wear—one with a sweetheart neckline, and the other with a one-shoulder strap—but they were all the same color and very similar. Providing a little diversity but still uniform for the pictures. I have also been to weddings where every bridesmaid has the same style dress, but a different color. It really is up to you on what you want your bridesmaids to wear, but it is an excellent idea to communicate with the bridesmaids and listen to their opinions about the dress. They are the ones who have to wear it, so you want to make sure they are comfortable.

My worst bridesmaid dress shopping experience was when my friend had gone to the bridal shop with one of her bridesmaids first, and then, a few weeks later, the rest of us went. Four of the six bridesmaids piled in the car for an afternoon of bridesmaid dress shopping. The bride thought she had picked out the dress she wanted us all to wear.

She thought, *Oh, this will just be a quick trip, you guys will try on the dress I have picked out and order your size, no big deal.* Oh, was she wrong. When I put on the dress she had picked out, oh my gosh, it looked terrible! I had never felt so uncomfortable in a dress before.

Even the sales associate told me, "Girl, you do not look good in that dress."

You know you don't look good when the sales associate tells you that you look bad. While I greatly appreciated the honesty, it certainly did nothing for my self-esteem.

"Emily, I know this is your wedding day, and you had this dress in mind, but can we please at least try on a few other dresses before making the final decision?" I asked.

Emily was very reluctant at first. She had selected this dress, and when Emily is set on something, it is hard for her to change her mind.

I then told her, "Emily, I will wear whatever you want me to wear, it is your day, but I do not feel comfortable in this dress, and even the sales associate told me I look bad. Do you really want me standing up beside you feeling so uncomfortable and looking terrible? If this is the dress you have your heart set on, then, I will wear it, but let's at least look at a few other options."

Luckily, I was able to talk with Emily and convince her to let us try on a few different dresses, and we found one that looked better on all of us. We each picked out a style or two and tried them on and discussed as a group which one we liked best. Emily got the final say, but by allowing the bridesmaids to be part of the decision-making process and try on multiple styles of dresses made a huge difference.

Also, why in the world are bridesmaid dresses made out of that terrible, shiny material? No one looks good in that. Although, in recent years, I have seen a shift, and more and more bridesmaids are wearing chiffon dresses that look a little more appealing. I understand the day is all about the bride, but if you want your friends to stand beside you and support you on your big day, then, you want to make sure they feel comfortable in their dresses too.

Yes to the Dress

While bridesmaid dress shopping maybe a bit of a struggle, wedding dress shopping should be a lot of fun! Wedding dress shopping can either be a fantastic experience or torture. When you are ready to go wedding dress shopping, go with an open mind and try not to get too worked up if you don't find the perfect dress the first time you go shopping. I have heard so many stories of girls who think they know exactly what type of dress they want, and then, when they get to the store, they hate it. Don't get worked up if you don't like most the dresses you try on. There are thousands of dresses to choose from, and you will find the perfect dress.

As you are keeping an open mind during the dress shopping process, also listen to the sales associate. While not all sales associates are good at their job, the majority are, and they do this for a living. So if they have a suggestion, listen to them; just because you try on a dress does not mean you have to buy that particular dress.

Also, be mindful of how many people you bring with you when you go dress shopping. Everyone will have an opinion, and sometimes, that makes it harder for you to make a decision. Go with your gut. Find a dress that you feel comfortable in and don't worry about what others think. Take one to three closest family members or friends and don't allow yourself to be influenced by others.

Hair and Makeup

The day has come, and you have all your girls together to get ready. I have fond memories of all of us girls laughing, eating some snacks, drinking champagne, and getting ready on the big wedding day.

Depending on your venue will determine where you will all get ready. I have been in weddings that we all went to the salon to get our hair and makeup done and then straight to the venue to get dressed. I have also been in weddings where the hairdressers and makeup artists come to us at the bride's house. It really does not make a difference; it will really be up to what is most convenient, cost-effective, and available.

Every wedding I have been in, there has always been a time crunch, and someone does not like the way their hair is done and wants it redone. Then, there is that one bridesmaid who ends up being last on the list and does not get to get her hair done professionally. No matter where you get ready, make sure you have enough hairstylists and makeup artists to get to everyone with plenty of time. You would be surprised how long it takes to get a group of girls ready for a wedding. Plan more time than you think you will need.

Don't Forget to Eat

During the morning and afternoon, while everyone is getting ready, make sure everyone is eating plenty of food and drinking water. I know, I know, you all feel like you are squeezing yourself into a tiny dress and don't want to eat anything, but it is imperative that you eat and drink plenty of fluids throughout the day.

The wedding day is typically a long day. You are getting up early to get ready, take pictures, and get to the ceremony on time. By the time you get to the reception and get to eat, it will be hours later. The last thing you want is to be starving and pass out during the ceremony because you did not eat or drink enough earlier in the day. Stay hydrated, but make sure you use the bathroom before the ceremony begins. Some good snacks to have around during the day are almonds, peanut butter crackers, and protein bars.

Getting to the Wedding

The day of Catherine's wedding, we were all getting ready, things were going well, and all of a sudden, Catherine's mom comes to get me with a worried look on her face.

We go to the other room, and she tells me, "The limo bus that is supposed to be here in fifteen minutes is broken down, and we now don't have a ride to the church."

She was so worried and did not know what to do. The groom's mother was the one taking care of the limo bus, and she kept calling Catherine's mom in a panic. Catherine's mom did not want to tell Catherine because she did not want to get her upset on her wedding day. One by one, all the bridesmaids heard the news, and we put a plan in place. Enough vehicles/drivers were secured, and we would all get to the church on time, just not as we planned.

Through all the whispers and, then, the groom's father and Catherine's grandparents showing up at the house, Catherine started to get anxious. She did not know what was going on.

Finally, when her mom walked in the room to tell her the bad news about the limo bus, Catherine said, "Did someone die?"

We all started laughing, and her mom said, "Oh, no, everyone is fine. The limo bus is just broken down."

When Catherine heard that it was just the limo bus, she took a big sigh of relief. She did not let a little thing like the limo bus breaking down and the need to change the transportation plan ruin her big day!

We all made it to the church on time, and it was a beautiful wedding. By the end of the ceremony, the limo bus company claimed the bus was fixed, and they were able to pick us up and take us to the reception. Little did we know they lied. The bus was not broken down, just the air conditioning. It was a very *hot* ride to the reception. Once again, the bride stayed calm and did not let a little heat ruin her day. She was now married and did not care. Lucky for us, we packed a bridal survival kit packed with deodorant and perfume, so we could all freshen up before entering into the reception.

Bride and Groom Gifts

Some of the extra things I have seen that make getting ready very special is when the bride and groom exchange gifts or when the bridesmaids give a gift to the bride. It is such an emotional day, but these little touches make a lasting impression and something that will be cherished for years to come.

For one wedding I was in, the bridesmaids asked all the influential women in the bride's life to make one scrapbook page, and then, we put it all together to present to the bride the day of the wedding. After getting her hair and makeup done, we presented her with the scrapbook.

Bad timing on our part; she started to open it and was about to cry and did not want to mess up her makeup, so she decided to wait to look at it all until after the wedding. It might be a good idea to present the gifts before the bride gets all ready, so if there are tears, she does not mess up her freshly done makeup. The scrapbook was something that was not hard for the bridesmaids to put together and not very expensive but meant so much to the bride. These little touches can make a huge impact.

I also really love seeing when the bride and groom exchange wedding gifts the day of the wedding. While I did not get to see the groom open his gift, I saw my friend open her gift, and I will never forget the expression on her face. This couple is truly in love, and I loved seeing my friend so happy and excited to marry the love of her life.

What made it even better was the photographer was informed of the exchange of the gifts, and he was able to take pictures of the bride opening her gift while she was surrounded by her bridesmaids getting ready and pictures of the groom opening his gift with his groomsmen. This, then, allowed the bride and groom to "see" the other person opening each other's gifts later and relive the moment with each other.

The day of the wedding is an exciting and emotional day. Being surrounded by your closest friends on this day makes a big difference.

Lessons:

- Select bridesmaids who are genuine friends. Girls that are going to be there for you and support you throughout the whole process.
- Be realistic with your expectations for your bridesmaids.
- Watch out for bridezilla tendencies.
- Don't purchase your bridal gown or bridesmaid dresses too early.
- On the day of the wedding, ensure you plan enough time for all the girls to get ready before the ceremony.
- Transportation—make sure you have a plan in place for getting to and from the ceremony and reception and have a plan *B*, just in case.
- Don't panic or get worked up if something goes wrong.

- Be considerate of the men and women you have asked to support you and be in your wedding. Everything costs a lot, so be mindful of expectations.
- Special touches like a gift for the bride or the couple exchanging gifts makes for an extra special memory.

Notes:

_____
_____
_____
_____
_____
_____
_____
_____
_____
_____
_____
_____
_____
_____
_____
_____
_____
_____
_____
_____
_____
_____
_____
_____
_____
_____
_____
_____
_____

The Guest List

I remember my friend and I drove to the wedding together, and when we arrived, I had said, "I think I am going to leave my coat in the car." She turned to me and said, "Hannah, the wedding is outside, you need to wear your coat!" I was shocked; I had no idea the wedding was outside and was certainly not dressed for an outside wedding in November.

How to Create the Guest List

The guest list will be one of the most stressful parts of the planning process. This is the part when you realize how much the wedding is not just about you. Your family and your fiancé's family will all have an opinion about who should be invited to the wedding. Before you start making your guest list have a good discussion with your partner and decide how many people you realistically want at the wedding. Your budget and the size of the venue will also play a part into how many guests you really can invite.

If you want a small wedding, then know that some people's feelings may get hurt, and that is okay. Not everyone can be invited to the wedding. There are no set standards of who has to be invited.

It is your day, so invite who you want to celebrate with you. While your parents and your partner's parents will also have guests they want to invite, you will need to set some parameters on the guest list to ensure only the people you want there are invited.

On more than one occasion, I have had friends come to me in a panic and worried about the guest list. They want to please everyone but also want the wedding of their dreams. One of the best things I have seen is to have a discussion with your partner first and make a game plan. Start making a quick preliminary list of the first friends and family that come to mind. Once you have that list, then, add twenty guests for your parent's friends and twenty guests for your fiancé's parent's friends. Now, you have a rough number of how many guests you want to invite. Don't overthink it.

While, many times, both sets of parents might be helping to fund some or all of the wedding, don't allow them to manipulate you into inviting people to your wedding you do not want. You have given them twenty guests to invite. Allow them to invite whoever they want—within reason—for those twenty spots, but nothing more. This will allow your parents to feel like they get some say, but you are still in control. If you don't set parameters, then, the guest list will get out of control, and before you know it, the butcher, the mailman, and everyone else in town will be invited.

Save the Dates

Once you have your guest list finalized, you can begin sending save-the-dates. "As a general rule, its best to start spreading the news around six to eight months prior to the ceremony, even earlier for a faraway destination or holiday weekend" (save-the-date etiquette). Sending out "save-the-dates" helps increase the chances of your guests actually attending the wedding. Sending them out six to eight months prior allows your guests time to plan accordingly and make a decision about their RSVP prior to actually receiving the invitation.

You are not required to send a save-the-date to every guest on your list. I would recommend setting up a tiered system for your guest list, that is if you have more people on your list than the number of guests you actually want to attend. Statistically, about 10 to 20 percent of the guests on your list will RSVP no, so it is a good idea to send out about 10 to 15 percent more invitations than the number of guests you truly want to attend. But if your guest list is larger than 20 percent of how many guests you actually want to attend, then you might want to consider a tiered system.

For a tiered system, you break up your guest list into three tiers—A, B, C. The A tier are the friends and family who you absolutely want at your wedding, no questions asked. Then, you go through the list again, and you decide who you really want at the wedding but would not be heartbroken if they don't come. That's the B tier. The last tier, the C tier, are the guests that you would like to invite, but really okay if they do not get invited. This might be friends that you were close to a long time ago, but have since drifted, or second cousins that you don't really know but feel obligated to invite.

Once you have divided up your guest list into the three tiers and you are now comfortable with the number of guests in the A and B tier, you can start sending out your save-the-dates. Everyone in the A tier will get the save-the-date, because of course, these are all the people you really want to attend the wedding. Having more guest spots available will depend on if you send any save-the-dates to guests in the B tier. You can pick and choose who in the B tier gets a save-the-date.

Next, when it is time to send the invitations, you send invitations to everyone in the A and B tier, once again knowing that about 10 to 20 percent will RSVP no. Once you start getting a few "nos" back, you can send some invitations out to your C tier. Keep in mind you don't want to wait too long to send additional invitations to your C tier guests. Be considerate of your guests and provide them enough time to RSVP by the deadline.

What Information Should Go on the Invitation

When you get ready to send the invitations, make sure you make it very clear on the invitation if your guests get a plus one and if children are invited to the wedding. While no matter how clear you have it on the invitation, you will still get a few people calling to invite their new girlfriend or boyfriend or just show up with their children, thinking the whole family is invited.

If you know the name of your friend's plus one, you should put their name on the invitation. If you do not know their name but still want to offer a plus one, then, you should address the invitation with their name and "guest." When sending invitations to friends or family with children, all guest's names should be addressed on the invitation if they are invited. If you do not want children at the wedding, then, be sure to include this information on the invitation or the wedding website. Or you can always have a separate conversation with your guests with children to ensure they know no children are invited to the wedding. As someone who does not have any children, I don't understand why anyone would want to bring their child as their date to a wedding. Leave the kids at home and enjoy a night out!

If you are not sure your guests will follow instructions, and you really do not want them to bring a plus one or their children, then, you should simply fill in the RSVP card with the number of guests you have allotted for them. If the invitation is only for them and no plus one, then on the RSVP card that they will send back, write in the number *1*. This should help eliminate any confusion. But don't be surprised if some people still call and ask for a plus one even though you have made it so clear.

"Do not pencil your significant other's name onto the RSVP card, and do not call and ask the bride for a plus one. 'It is just beyond not okay,' Post said, adding that it's one of the top ten complaints she gests from couples. 'Once the bride and groom have come to their decision, it is what it is. Asking them to change is disrespectful, and it puts them in an awkward position'" (Bindley 2011).

As you can imagine, there are a lot of details that go into planning a wedding. For some people, details are not their thing at all. If you and your fiancé are both not detail people, you might want to consider enlisting some help in planning your wedding from friends and family or paying a wedding planner. There are so many details that are needed to pull off a fabulous wedding to ensure you and your guests have a great time. You want to provide your guests with all the required information for them to enjoy the wedding day. This will also help eliminate all the crazy phone calls and text messages the week of the wedding from your guests. You will be busy enough the week of the wedding; you don't need to be dealing with guests asking basic questions about the day. While you may not be able to put everything on the invitation itself, by creating a wedding website and putting the link on the invitation, you can provide your guests with all the necessary information about the wedding. The wedding website should be the place for your guests to find all the answers.

There is nothing that bothers me more about weddings than not having all the necessary information. I went to a wedding once in the month of November in Maryland that was outside, and I had no idea it was outside until I arrived.

I remember my friend and I drove to the wedding together, and when we arrived, I had said, "I think I am going to leave my coat in the car."

She turned to me and said, "Hannah, the wedding is outside, you need to wear your coat!"

I was shocked; I had no idea the wedding was outside and was certainly *not* dressed for an outside wedding in November.

I don't know if you know this or not, but November is cold in Maryland. This was not the only time this has happened. I attended another wedding that I did not know it was outside until the day before. I started looking up the venue and saw all these pictures of weddings outside, and I realized that their ceremony was probably outside. I texted a friend to confirm, and sure enough, this wedding was outside.

Before sending your wedding invitations, be sure to provide information about the ceremony and reception and please include if it is an outside wedding.

Speaking of information to include in the invitations, it is always helpful to include directions to the venue. There is nothing worse than trying to get to a wedding and getting lost.

* * * * *

"Hey, gang, it is time to load up the car and head to the wedding," Peter said.

Sam's wedding was about an hour away, and I decided to ride with a friend and her family to the wedding. We were driving along, following the GPS, and made a few turns off the interstate.

Peter, who was driving, thought we were pretty close to the wedding venue. The GPS starts going in and out, losing service.

"Kim, can you please look up the direction on your phone? Something does not seem right," asked Peter.

Kim tried to Google the directions, but her cell service went out. Peter made a few more turns, thinking he was going the right direction, and we ended up at a dead-end.

"Oh, man! This certainly isn't it," Kim said.

"Well, duh," said Peter. Peter turned back around and was starting to get frustrated at this point.

The GPS and cell phones still did not work.

"I think I saw a small store a little way back. Maybe, we can ask them for directions?" Kim said.

Peter, all frustrated, said, "I've got this, I am sure we can find our way."

After twenty minutes of driving around, making wrong turns, and continuing to get lost, Peter finally drove back to the small store, and Kim ran in to ask for directions. "Guys, we are so close!" Kim exclaimed.

We were only two short turns away from the wedding venue driveway; we just did not know it. Now feeling a little motion sick and Peter very frustrated, we all piled out of the car and headed to the wedding. We were all ready to hit the bar after that excursion.

* * * * *

In this day and age, I don't know anyone who actually prints out directions anymore before traveling, so it is always helpful to provide basic directions in the invitation or wedding website if your venue is in a remote location or not easily accessible, to help your guests arrive at the venue on time and in good spirits. I am so glad I decided to ride with some friends to this wedding; otherwise, I don't think I ever would have gotten there.

Along with directions to the venue, it is helpful to include parking information if it is not easy and convenient. When selecting your venue, this is something you will want to keep in mind, as parking can be a big headache for people. Depending on the venue, parking may be easy and free, or it could be a challenge and cost your guests money. I have found that weddings that are at a location that has plenty of easy parking provide a stress-free arrival for your guests.

For Susan's wedding, she had the ceremony at a church in the county, and then, we had to drive to the reception venue which was in the city. Susan did a great job ensuring all guests were aware of the multiple locations and provided directions from the ceremony to the reception, but I did not know there would be limited parking at the reception venue.

This particular venue in the city only had street parking. I circled around for what seemed like forever to try and find a spot to park. Once I finally found a place, I had to pay for parking. Unfortunately, by the time I got to the reception, I was a bit frustrated and had wished the parking situation was different. It would have been helpful if the bride and groom provided a shuttle service to and from the reception venue or to and from a nearby parking garage, so all the guests did not have to fight for limited parking spaces. While I do understand this is an extra expense, little touches like a shuttle make a huge difference in your guest's experience.

Taren's wedding was in the city, and the invitation directed people to park in the attached garage of the hotel venue, and then the bride and groom provided parking vouchers and paid for our parking. This was undoubtedly the best approach when there is a cost to parking. Your guests are already traveling to attend your wedding, buying you a gift, and giving up their time to celebrate you; the least you can do is take care of them and pay for their parking. Extra touches that enhance the arrival experience would be to provide a parking attendant and/or a door attendant to help direct your guests. The whole point is you want your guests to have a smooth arrival experience so that they can enjoy the rest of the evening.

Wedding Invitation Etiquette

Another aspect of ensuring your guests have all the needed information is to make sure everyone gets an invitation. While I understand, we live in a very electronic-, social media-, and email-driven world, but when it comes to your wedding, do not send electronic invitations.

* * * * *

"Hey, Hannah, I just got a message from Emily on Facebook. You are invited to her wedding," Erika, my college roommate, yelled down the hallway.

"What!" I exclaimed.

"Yeah, Emily sent out wedding invitations via Facebook last week," Erika said.

"Well, I am not on Facebook right now," I said.

"I know. That is why Emily just sent me a message. She realized you did not get the Facebook invite and wanted to make sure I shared it with you because you are invited," Erika explained.

Clearly, we were not that close of friends that Emily could not call, text, or talk to me in person to invite me to her wedding herself. This was, by far, the worst type of invitation I had ever received.

Spend the time and money and send real invitations to all your guests. Along with the invitation, inform your guests where you are registered. See chapter 13 for more information on wedding registry etiquette.

I was invited to one wedding that the invitation said formal ceremony and casual reception. The couple indicated that people could bring a change of clothes for the reception but wanted everyone to be very formal for the ceremony. I then got to the ceremony, and the groom and groomsmen were all dressed in jeans and a vest. The setting was not formal either. There was no reason to indicate that the ceremony was formal when the whole thing was pretty casual.

Although, it was nice that the couple did indicate the type of attire their guests should wear. Sometimes, it can be difficult to know what to wear if you are not familiar with the venue. My advice is to always err on the side of overdressed than underdressed. The worst is when you do not realize the wedding is outside, and you are have not dressed appropriately for an outside wedding. Do your homework or ask questions before the week of the wedding, so you know what to expect when you arrive.

The guest list and sending out the invitations will be one of the worst parts of the planning process. Really think through your guest list, create a tiered system if needed, and don't stress about hurting people's feelings. Don't allow the guest list to overwhelm you; this is your day, and you get to decide who celebrates with you.

Lessons:

- The guest list will be stressful but make a game plan and stick to the list.
- Allow your parents and your fiancé's parents to invite twenty guests each.
- If your guest list is too extensive, create an *ABC* tier system for sending out the save-the-dates and invitations.
- Details are most important; make sure all necessary information is on the invitation or wedding website.
- Mail real invitations to all your guests; do not send electronic wedding invitations.

- Be prepared for awkward conversations with your guests regarding their RSVPs and asking to bring a plus one or their children.
- Specify the type of attire you are expecting from your guests especially if it is outside or a particular type of venue that requires an attire different than typical wedding attire.

Notes:

_____
_____
_____
_____
_____
_____
_____
_____
_____
_____
_____
_____
_____
_____
_____
_____
_____
_____
_____
_____
_____
_____
_____
_____
_____
_____
_____
_____
_____
_____
_____

Music and Entertainment

Oh, was I wrong. Of course, my brother is much stronger than I am, and he saw what I was doing. So instead of bumping into me lightly or letting me shove him, I went flying across the dance floor. I was inches away from knocking over the speaker which would have fallen into a glass window. To make it worse, I landed right near the long line for the bar. Everyone saw me go flying, so I quickly jumped up, pretended like I "stuck the landing," and hopped in line for a drink. Everyone in line and on the dance floor cheered!

Find a Good DJ or Band

The music can make or break how much fun your guests have at your wedding. Like it or not, your wedding is not just about you. Your wedding is a celebration of the commitment you and your partner are vowing to each other, but a simple commitment could be done at the courthouse. A wedding is a celebration with your family and friends, and while it is about you, it is essential to keep your guests in mind when planning your wedding!

The thing I remember most about each wedding is the music and the dancing. I love to dance, and if I can't spend the majority of the reception on the dance floor, then, I probably did not have a great time at your wedding.

I will never forget at Lucy's wedding, I was with my whole family, and I was on the dance floor with my brother and sister. My younger brother, who is much taller than me, started going back-and-forth, bumping into my sister and me who were on either side. My sister decided she did not want to be a part of these shenanigans and moved out of the way so he can't keep bumping into her. I, on the other hand, decide to lower my shoulder and think I can shove my brother back.

Oh, was I wrong. Of course, my brother is much stronger than I am, and he saw what I was doing. So instead of bumping into me lightly or letting me shove him, I went flying across the dance floor. I was inches away from knocking over the speaker which would have fallen into a glass window. To make it worse, I landed right near the long line for the bar. Everyone saw me go flying, so I quickly jumped up, pretended like I "stuck the landing," and hopped in line for a drink. Everyone in line and on the dance floor cheered!

It was a bit embarrassing, but worse than that is it really hurt. I landed on my arm in a funny way, and my elbow then hurt for the next whole year. I still give my brother a hard time about that night to this day.

* * * * *

Lucy's wedding was the wedding that everyone was having so much fun that a bunch of the guests put money together and paid the DJ to stay an extra hour after the bride and groom left. We were all having so much fun and did not want the party to end. You know it is a good wedding when no one wants to go home.

Having an excellent DJ or band that can get everyone on the dance floor really makes a big difference. At Scott's wedding, they had the reception outside in a big tent. We all ate, and then, the DJ got everyone on the dance floor. The DJ was so engaging and really encouraged everyone to dance. He started the evening playing songs that all generations would enjoy and could dance to, and then, as the night went on, after many of the older people left, he geared the music to the younger crowd, and we had a blast. By the end of the night, there were keg stands and pitchers of beer passed around, and everyone sharing some pie without utensils. This DJ was fantastic and really knew how to entertain the crowd and ensure everyone had a great time.

Brittany's wedding also had a great DJ. This was a DJ couple that brought props like glow sticks and hats and noisemakers for the dance floor. The props added a whole other layer of entertainment for the guests. The one DJ also did a little karaoke during the night as well. Many people at the wedding enjoyed the bar a bit too much, and this DJ knew how to entertain the crowd and ensure everyone had a fantastic time. Many guests at this wedding were older and not into dancing but still enjoyed the evening.

Unfortunately, I have also been to weddings when the music is not so great. Claire and her fiancé, James, were not very big into dancing, so they decided to add a lot of other unique things besides the father-daughter dance and mother-son dance into the reception and had a limited time for guest dancing. They included a twenty-minute slideshow, various speeches, and the dance when all the couples get on the floor, and dance until the couple that has been together the longest is the last on the dance floor. For them, this worked, and they enjoyed the special dances and things with their family, but for the guests, it was not as entertaining.

The DJ needs to be able to get the crowd on the dance floor as soon as possible. Dim the lights and get the party started as people are finishing their dinner. You do not have to wait until everyone is done eating and all the "formal, traditional stuff" is done before you start the dancing. If you do not get people up on the dance floor early, they will start leaving. Most people do not want to come to a wedding and sit at their table for hours, watching slideshows and hearing speeches. They want to interact with the other guests, dance, and have fun.

Wedding Games

I have seen a couple of wedding games incorporated into the reception that can be entertaining for the guests. One game I saw a couple of times that seems to entertain the guests is a fun, simple version of the newlywed game. Two chairs are placed in the center of the dance floor back-to-back. The bride and groom each take off their shoes and give one to the other person and keep one for them. They sit down with their backs facing each other, and the DJ or MC asks the couple questions such as, "Who is the better driver," or "Who is the messiest?" After each question, the bride and groom raise the appropriate shoe of who they think matches the question. This is always so comical to watch and provides some lighthearted entertainment for the guests.

If you are going to add games or other entertainment into your reception, I would suggest only add one extra thing and do it early in the evening. If you can, time it with the service of the food. If you have a plated meal, play the game while the first course is being served or in between the first and second course to allow people to focus on something else other than the food service. It can be hard to serve a large group all at once, and it takes time, so if you can find ways to entertain your guests during this time and then let them enjoy their meal, it adds a nice flow to the evening. This also allows all the time after the meal for dancing!

Photo Booth

One thing I do enjoy that has started to become more popular is to have a photo booth. Many DJs or entertainment companies now offer packages with photo booths. This is a great, fun way to capture the evening and provide something to keep your guests entertained when they take a break from the dance floor.

One idea I really like is when the photo booth provides two copies of the pictures; one for you to keep, and the other for you to put in a book and leave a message for the couple. This is a fun alternative to a guest book and captures the excitement of the evening. It is also nice when the company then provides a digital copy of all the pictures taken that night for the couple. I am sure there are lots of different packages these companies offer, but this is one example that I think is a great addition to the reception and provides lasting memories for the couple. While you will undoubtedly have plenty of professional "staged" photos, it is nice to get funny, spontaneous photos from a photo booth.

Do your research and find out what your entertainment company can provide. Many times, you can save money by bundling packages with one company verse having a different company for each item. But this all depends on what you are looking for and how much you want to spend. The options are literally endless. If you have it in your mind of what you want, I am confident there is a company that can provide the service.

Other things I have seen in regard to photography are providing disposable cameras on each table and allowing the guests to take pictures all throughout the night. The bride and groom then collect all the cameras and get the pictures printed and can relive the reception from each table's perspective and not just all the professional photos. Although, I am not convinced disposable cameras and developing film will be around much longer.

I have also seen couples who provide a wedding photo website for people to share all their pictures so everyone at the wedding can enjoy all photos taken. Now, with social media being so large and hashtags, I have seen many couples creating a fun hashtag for their wedding, and anyone sharing photos on social media is encouraged to use that hashtag, so everyone can enjoy the pictures.

Avoid Asking Friends to Work the Wedding

One thing that I have seen too often and something to keep in mind when planning is to be very cautious of asking friends to provide services for the reception. Having a DJ who is your friend sounds like a fantastic idea, and you think you will save money, but you might want to think twice before hiring friends to DJ at your wedding.

At one of the weddings I have been to, the DJ was the groom's good friend. He was charging the couple very minimal for his time and service but wanted to enjoy the wedding while working. During the cocktail hour, he pounded back a few cocktails before his primary duties in the reception started, and by the time it was time to introduce the bridal party, he was wasted. He slurred his words, presented each person individually instead of two at a time as lined up, and took way too long to switch the songs and get everyone in the room.

Then, as the evening went on, he tried to get more drinks from the bar, but the bartenders were instructed by their boss not to serve him anymore. The DJ started to get angry and then, of course, informed the bride and groom and caused an enormous ruckus.

My advice would be don't ask friends to provide services for your wedding unless they fully understand that they are working the wedding and not attending. Spend the money on a professional and let your friends enjoy the evening.

Band versus DJ

I have been to only a couple of weddings that have had a band instead of a DJ. I like a DJ more than a band, but the weddings that had a band turned out great. With a band, you are limited to similar music throughout the evening and limited to what music the band knows. With a DJ, you can request anything, and most likely, the DJ will be able to play it. I have also found that with a band, it is sometimes harder to understand their lyrics versus a DJ playing the music from the original artist.

You will also need to consider your venue and space which might help you decide. If your reception location is not very large, they might not have enough room for a full band to set up and play throughout the ceremony and/or reception. Another thing to keep in mind is the cost. Generally, a DJ will cost less than a band. "Although prices will vary, a good wedding DJ can cost between $600 and $1,200, and a good live band can cost between $1,500 and $10,000" (Band vs. DJ).

Alternate Reception Ideas

No matter what type of music you decide, having good music throughout the reception makes a huge difference and helps set the tone for your guests. One alternative reception idea that one of my friends did was having the dancing part of their reception at a dance club. They had a small wedding at a church and then a dinner reception in a private room at a local restaurant. After the dinner, they invited everyone and more to a bar where there was music and dancing.

This was a fabulous alternative to an expensive reception. The bride and groom had a great time and got to celebrate their big day with their family and friends but did not have the stress and pressure of putting on a full reception with DJ and all. One thing they also did, which I loved, was provided a bunch of disposable cameras for people at the bar. They gave out the cameras and asked people to take pictures throughout the night. This was such a fun idea, and they ended up with some great photos. Once again, this was an excellent alternative to a traditional, formal photographer.

Your wedding is your day, and the sky is the limit to what you can add to the reception to make it most enjoyable. Keep your guests in mind and have fun with the planning. Do your research and decide on what type of music, photographer, and games will make the evening most festive and entertaining for all parties involved.

Lessons:

- Music and getting your attendees dancing is a must.
- Keep your guests in mind when planning.
- Remove the slideshow from the program.
- Photo booths add a new level of entertainment for your guests and provide great pictures to capture the evening.
- There are alternative ways to have a fun party without paying a fortune.
- Don't ask your friends to work at the wedding if they want to fully enjoy the festivities.

Notes:

_____

_____

_____

_____

_____

_____

_____

_____

_____

_____

_____

_____

_____

_____

_____

_____

_____

_____

_____

_____

_____

_____

_____

_____

_____

_____

_____

_____

_____

_____

_____

_____

_____

_____

Don't Forget the Rings

We are nearing the end of the ceremony, and the officiant asks the best man for the rings. The look on the best man's face was priceless. He suddenly realized he did not have the rings. Everyone at first thought he was just joking, but he was mortified.

Keep Calm and Don't Become a Bridezilla

We have all heard those stories of weddings that just did not go the way they were planned or that crazy bride who was so demanding she lost all her friends. Well, I have firsthand experience with this type of wedding. From the very beginning, I knew we were going to run into issues. If you know anyone with a type *A* personality, you know that they have to have everything their way, and it has to be perfect.

As you can imagine, planning a wedding is not an easy task, and as time gets closer and closer to the big day, many brides become a bit unglued. Emotions are high; the bride wants everything to be perfect and, many times, expect far too much from their friends and family during this time. I am sure you are familiar with the term "bridezilla," defining the crazy, high-demanding, "everything has to be my way" bride, as they are planning and preparing for the big wedding day.

One thing that can help with a bridezilla the day of the wedding is to ensure all the details are in place and stay calm. If something goes wrong the day of the wedding, relax and know that it will be okay. It is very easy to get worked up and upset when something goes wrong, but it is just not worth it. While your wedding is the most important day of your life, it is also only one day of your life. Things will go wrong, but if you play it off in a calm manner, you may be the only person that actually knows. But if you throw a fit or cause a scene, everyone will know, and it makes things so much worse. Stay calm and enjoy your day.

Always Know Where the Rings Are

A critical detail before the wedding ceremony begins is to make sure the best man actually has the rings. At Shannon's wedding, the best man, David, forgot the rings. The father of the groom, Bob, was officiating the wedding, and both of the groom's brothers were part of the bridal party, with David being the best man.

When it came the time in the ceremony for the rings, Bob turned to David—who is very much a jokester—and asked for the rings. "May I have the rings please?"

The look on David's face was priceless. He had a sense of panic and quickly began checking his pockets.

David turned to his younger brother and asked, "Do you have the rings?"

Through this process, everyone thought David was playing a joke.

Bob finally said, "All right, enough is enough. Please give me the rings."

With the feeling of disappointment in his voice, he quickly whispered to his dad, "I don't have the rings, I forgot them in the car."

David quickly ran back to the dressing room and grabbed his keys to fetch the rings. Little did he know that he would get locked out of the church and have to run around to a door on the other end of the building. It literally took like fifteen minutes for him to get the rings. Talk about an awkward few minutes. Meanwhile, Bob began to tell jokes and kept everyone entertained, but of course, us bridesmaids were not very amused. It was hot, our feet hurt, and we just wanted to sit down. While this absolutely is not something you would want to happen at your wedding, it made a great story.

To prohibit this from happening to you, ensure that you have a checklist of all necessary items for the ceremony and have a key person in charge to be sure that all the elements are in place and ready for the ceremony. Luckily, both the bride and groom were lighthearted about this situation and did not cause a scene during the ceremony, but because emotions are high during this time, you would never want to test the bride and forget the rings. Shannon did a great job of keeping her cool during the ceremony, but as you can imagine, she was not very happy.

Wedding Programs

One thing that I have noticed that gets forgotten a lot is to have someone hand out the programs. On more than one occasion, I have gotten a last-minute phone call the day before the wedding to ask if I can hand out programs. Apparently, this is something people tend to overlook. The couple will select their groomsmen and bridesmaids, decide if they will have anyone speak or sing at the wedding, and choose their friends for those roles, but they will not think about the programs.

Many couples will work with the officiant of the wedding to create the details of the ceremony and then have a program printed for their guests. They take the time to create the program and then don't think about who will hand out the programs the day of the wedding. I have seen where the couple just have the ushers hand them out or have one person at the entrance instructing guests to sign the guestbook and grab a program. But as I mentioned, on two different occasions, I got that last-minute call to hand out programs. These are those little details that sometimes get forgotten. I, of course, loved to be a part of the day and was glad to jump in and help.

I certainly would not spend a lot of time or money creating a program for the ceremony. Most people have been to a wedding before, and ceremonies are pretty similar. A program can be a nice touch to give your guests an outline of the ceremony and let them know who everyone is in the bridal party, but it is definitely not necessary. A wedding I recently attended had a large sign at the entrance of the ceremony with the timeline of the evening, very similar to the information in a program. This sign fit with her theme, provided the guests the needed information, and saved time and money on not making individual programs for each guest. The programs get thrown away right after the ceremony, so don't waste the money if you are on a budget.

The Processional

This may sound like a simple concept, but during the rehearsal of the ceremony, practice walking down the aisle properly. The day of the wedding, everyone is a bit nervous, but you don't want to be walking like a duck down the aisle. There are lots of different options for the processional and how everyone gets into the ceremony. Some people choose to have the best man and groomsmen walk in with the officiant and groom first while others decide just to have the groom and best man walk in with the officiant or only the groom and officiant. It is up to the couple and what makes them feel comfortable.

If it is just the groom and officiant who walk in the front together, then, the groomsmen will all be paired with bridesmaids and walk down the aisle together. The groomsmen should be on the right and the bridesmaid on the left. Each couple should attach arms and walk slowly down the aisle. The bridesmaid holds the bouquet with two hands at waist level. The order of the bridesmaids and groomsmen should be determined before the rehearsal, and they will walk in from the furthest away from the couple to the closest with the maid of honor and best man last.

If all of the groomsmen walk in with the groom, then the bridesmaids would walk down the aisle by themselves. Once again, they walk with their hands together, holding their flower bouquet low about waist level. They should walk at an even pace, not too fast and not too slow. You want to smile and make eye contact with the guests as you are walking down the aisle. You do not want to over-think it and take the giant awkward step slowly and then bring the rest of your body to meet your feet like a duck pecking at food. You want slow even steps all the way down the aisle.

The other option is a little mix of both when the groom and best man walk in together. All the bridesmaids and groomsmen walk in as pairs as mentioned before, and the maid of honor walks in on her own last before the flower girl—if there is one—or right before the bride.

Typically, the order of the procession for a Christian wedding starts with the grandparents escorted in before the start of the cer-emony, then the officiant, groom, and best man comes in from the side (or you can have just the groom or all groomsmen). Then, the mother and father of the groom walk down the aisle; then, the mother of the bride is escorted into the ceremony. Another son, a groomsman, an usher, or another man of your choosing can escort the mother of the bride. It is really up to the couple and the mother of the bride as to who will escort her into the ceremony. Then, the bridesmaids and groomsmen walk into the ceremony. If the couple decides to have a flower girl and/or ring bearer, then, they walk down the aisle, and then, it is time for the bride.

Traditionally, the father of the bride walks his daughter down the aisle. But I have been to plenty of weddings where the father of the bride does not have a good relationship or is no longer alive, and some-one else escorts the bride. Once again, this is really up to you and what you feel most comfortable with and who you want to give you away.

Unity Element

The majority of the weddings I have attended have been Christian weddings, and many will have some type of unity element to them, bringing the two families into one. These are not solely for Christian weddings; many nonreligious weddings may decide to include some type of unity element to their ceremony.

Some of the things I have seen are a unity candle, unity rope, sand, cross, painting, and wine box. These are certainly not required for your wedding but add an extra element to the ceremony. For the unity candle, there are typically two separate candles that the mothers of the bride and groom each light when they walk into the ceremony to be seated, and then, during the ceremony, the officiant will have the bride and groom take the lighted candles and light one large candle in the center. This is signifying two individuals are becoming one.

I have been to a couple of weddings that have used the unity candle, and the mothers of the bride and groom struggled to get the candle lit. They were nervous, and it took too long. A little trick to make sure the candles light quickly during the ceremony is to make sure all the brand-new candles have been lit at least once to make it easier to light during the ceremony. New candles typically take a couple of extra seconds to light whereas a candle that has been lit before will catch fire quicker.

At one wedding, when the mother of the bride lit her candle, she got nervous and was about to also light the unity candle in the center. A few people in the crowd yelled, "Nooo," and she quickly realized what she was doing and placed her candle where it needed to go.

The unity sand is very similar to the unity candle, except the mothers of the bride and groom do not partake. There are two individual containers of sand set out, typically two different colors, and then, during the ceremony, the bride and groom pour the sand into one large container. The sand can never be separated, signifying that the marriage is forever, and nothing should separate it.

The unity rope is three strands of rope tied at the top, and during the ceremony the couple braids the pieces of rope. Once again, it represents the two families becoming one, and a braid is durable and cannot be broken.

A few unique things I have seen in ceremonies are build-a-cross set that has an outer masculine frame and inner feminine cross, and the couple uses pegs to put it together. I have also seen a couple create a painting. As the mothers of the bride and groom are escorted into the wedding, they contribute to the painting, and then, the bride and groom finish off the painting, creating a heart shape.

One of my favorite things I have seen is a wine box. Prior to the wedding, the bride and groom both wrote a letter to each other. Then, during the ceremony, they read their letters and place them in the box along with a bottle of their favorite wine. They then nail the box shut. On their one-year anniversary, they are to write another letter and share it with their spouse and drink the bottle of wine. They can continue to do this year after year and have a box full of love letters.

I have also heard of couples doing this, and then, at their first fight, they open the box and wine and remember where it all started and how much they really love each other. Either way, this is a great thing to add to your special wedding day.

While many wedding ceremonies are similar, it is your day, and you get to make it your own. Add the special touches that you want and make it personal. My favorite ceremony was one that was pretty small and intimate. The couple did not want a huge wedding and only invited their closest friends and family. During the ceremony, they added a few very personal touches, wrote their vows, and the couple's personality really came through for their guests to share in their joy. It really was a special ceremony.

Decorations for the Ceremony

There are lots of different special touches you can add to the ceremony and, of course, various types of decorations. Typically, simple flowers or candles can be used for the ceremony to add a nice touch, but you really don't have to overdo it. Many times, the florist will use the same flowers from the ceremony for the reception. This is always a great idea and saves a little money.

If you are thinking about using floating candles down the aisle, you should seriously reconsider. I have been to a couple of weddings where the aisle is lined with glass jars of water and floating candles. Every time I have seen this, it was always a disaster. The ushers do their best to try and direct people to use the outside aisles to find their seats, but inevitably, someone always walks down the middle aisle and knocks over the candles, water goes everywhere, and it is a mess.

I have seen men's jackets nearly catch on fire, and the worst thing I have seen with these candles is after the flower girl had walked down the aisle, she sat down with her parents. The bride then walked down the aisle, and all of a sudden, the flower girl's dress was on fire. A few attendees, way in the back, saw what was happening but didn't want to make a big scene. Everyone was so focused on the father of the bride giving his daughter away that no one saw the smoke. Then, as the bride was walking up to grab hands with her groom, the officiant had a clear view and saw the flower girl's dress catch fire. He didn't want to cause a ruckus, but people were starting to wonder why he had such a weird look on his face and was trying to motion to the wedding coordinator in the back. Then, all of a sudden, the couple sitting a few rows behind the flower girl screamed, "FIRE!" Everyone began to panic.

Quickly, the wedding coordinator figured out that it was the flower girl's dress that is on fire and ran and threw her coffee that she had in her hand on the dress. The flower girl screamed and started to cry, causing a bit of a fiasco. The flower girl and her mom left the ceremony, so she could console her daughter. The wedding coordinator blew out the rest of the candles in the aisle, and then, the ceremony continued. Not exactly the wedding ceremony the bride and groom envisioned, but certainly one to remember. Hopefully, the little flower girl is not too scarred for life.

Timing

Typically, the ceremony should be about twenty to thirty minutes depending on how many "extras" you decide to add to the ceremony. Many couples like to have a reading or two from friends or a particular song sung. While the times can vary, typically, the shorter the better, but you don't want it too short. I was at one wedding where it took longer for the bridal party to walk into the ceremony than the ceremony itself. In my opinion, that was too short, but the couple wanted it short and sweet, so it worked for them.

On the flip side, you don't want it to be too long. Unless it is a formal Catholic ceremony, which is typically about an hour-long service, keep it to thirty minutes or less. At one of the weddings, the couple wanted to add so many special touches and incorporate more people into the ceremony with readings and songs that it was about an hour and a half ceremony which was way too long. No one wants to sit that long at a wedding ceremony. Make the ceremony special and unique, but don't overdo it. Your guests really don't want to sit through an hour-long ceremony. They really just want to get to the reception to eat, drink, dance, and have fun.

Speaking of the reception, the flow of the day and the venues you are using for the ceremony and reception will determine the timeline for the day. I have found it is always best to have the cocktail hour right after the ceremony and have that lead into the reception. While you might need a little time in between the ceremony and cocktail hour for travel, no one wants hours in between the ceremony and reception.

I was at one wedding where the couple decided to have a large gap in time between the ceremony and reception. The couple wanted to take a lot of pictures and did not want to have to leave the reception to take the pictures or have the guests waiting forever at the cocktail hour or reception for the bridal party to arrive. So instead of having everything flow one thing after another, they decided to put a two-hour break in between the ceremony and reception. This actually cut off the flow of the day for the guests and required them to find something to do during the downtime. Many guests were from out of town and did not know where to go and really felt like it was a waste of time. Some guests simply decided to just go home and not return for the reception.

Lessons:

- Plan as much as you can but know things will go wrong.
- Have a checklist for the day of the wedding to ensure nothing is forgotten.
- Don't spend a lot of time or money on creating programs for the ceremony. If you do decide to do programs, don't forget to ask someone to hand them out to the guests.
- Have a rehearsal for the ceremony and have everyone practice walking down the aisle.
- Keep a tight timeline with a twenty- to thirty-minute ceremony and the cocktail hour and reception right after.

Notes:

_____

_____

_____

_____

_____

_____

_____

_____

_____

_____

_____

_____

_____

_____

_____

_____

_____

_____

_____

_____

_____

_____

_____

_____

_____

_____

_____

_____

_____

_____

_____

_____

_____

The Perfect Venue

Picking out a venue can be a bit stressful for some couples. In the olden days, you typically married the girl or guy next door, and your parents threw you a wedding celebration, and the whole town was invited. There was not much traveling, and it was a simple ceremony and celebration at the church but not a multiday affair.

Wedding Venues

When selecting your wedding venue, the sky is the limit. I have seen inside weddings, outside weddings, formal, informal, city, and country. I have traveled to multiple states and even experienced foreign weddings in Saudi Arabia and Egypt. I have been to weddings at vineyards, near the water, hotels, country clubs, restaurants, and more. I have only been to two weddings that have used the same venue. Even though the weddings were at the same location, it was an entirely different experience based on the special touches and décor the couple provided as well as the guests attending the wedding. No two weddings are alike, and I enjoy something different about each one.

Before you can even begin to start searching for your perfect wedding venue, you need to have an estimated idea of how many people will be attending the wedding. While it is still very early, and you may have no idea how many people will actually attend your wedding, it is a good idea to think through realistically about how many people you want to invite. Come up with a rough guest list and decide about how many people you are thinking; this will certainly narrow down your venue search. If you want a wedding with two hundred and fifty guests, then, you will need a venue that can accommodate such a large wedding. If you want a small intimate wedding with fifty guests, then, you will not want to look at venues that only have large event space. Start with a tentative guest list, do your research online, and then, begin making appointments to visit venues.

Some of the details that make each wedding unique are the type of venue they choose and then how they set up the space. You will obviously work with the venue event coordinator, but being able to understand your guest's needs and your vision for your wedding helps the coordinator bring that vision to life, so you have the best experience possible for your big day.

Picking out a venue can be a bit stressful for some couples. In the olden days, you typically married the girl or guy next door, and your parents threw you a wedding celebration, and the whole town was invited. There was not much traveling, and it was a simple ceremony and celebration at the church but not a multiday affair. Now, people travel from all over to attend weddings. It typically becomes a whole weekend of festivities and is not just a simple small gathering of close friends and family who all live close by. With this change and the fact that the majority of your guests will need to travel to attend your wedding, when you are selecting your venue, you want to keep your guests in mind. "While getting married might be one of the most self-absorbed times in a person's life, you take into account any special accommodations your guests might need when selecting a venue" (Lord 2013).

I had one friend who wanted to get married in the city where she and her fiancé lived. Neither of them was from this city, so they knew both sides of their family would have to travel, and the majority of their friends would be traveling as well. As they were looking at venues, they had this in mind, so they started looking at hotels or places that were close to a hotel. They wanted to make the travel experience to their wedding as stress-free as possible. They also knew that they had a few family members that were in wheelchairs. This, of course, is an added obstacle, but it was important for them to find a venue that was extremely wheelchair accessible to ensure there was less stress for these guests.

The couple ended up picking a hotel for their ceremony and reception. They wanted everything to be in one spot, so no one had to get back in their car once they arrived and made it easy for traveling guests. Their ceremony was in one ballroom of the hotel, their cocktail hour in another area, and then, the reception in a different ballroom. All rooms were wheelchair accessible and easy to get to and from each room. This was a fantastic setup that really kept their guests in mind. To make it even better, there was an attached parking garage to the hotel, and the bride and groom paid for parking for their guests. Thinking through all the details of the venue and having an understanding of your guests makes a huge difference in the guests' experience.

I have talked to other friends as they have been searching for the perfect wedding venue and, of course, cost plays a significant impact on your decisions. Some couples have chosen their venue based on the fact that they could get the most "bang for their buck" at a particular venue. When selecting your venue, you will need to ask lots of questions and find out if it is a full-service or limited-service venue. Full-service venues typically provide all the necessary items you would need such as tables and chairs, linen, flatware, and centerpieces. While limited-service venues only offer the space, and you would need to coordinate with multiple vendors to fill the space and get everything you would need for the wedding. Some limited-service venues also have preferred vendors that you must use which then limits your ability to shop around and select vendors within your price range. Each type of venue has its advantages and disadvantages, and it is ultimately up to you on where you want to get married and your vision of what the reception should look like. No matter what type of venue you eventually decide on, you are still able to add some of your own signature special touches to make the day unique.

Room Setup and Seating Charts

Once you have selected your venue, you will work with the event coordinator to design the setup for the room. If you are anything like me, you will want a large dance floor. I have seen couples that want a large area for gifts, pictures, and guestbook signing or multiple bars in the room. All of these things take up space, and you have to figure out how many people you want at your wedding and how you want to fit everything into the space.

I have seen weddings that have round tables, rectangular tables, or a mix of both. I have also seen a *U*-shape with the dance floor in the middle. This particular bride had a vision in mind of what she wanted the reception to look like and did not want the traditional scattered tables around the room. She wanted it to be like a big family gathering and chose to do a *U*-shape.

Other things I have seen are having a head table for the entire bridal party or a sweetheart table for just the bride and groom. I personally am a fan of a head table with the whole bridal party, but it really is up to you and who all is in your bridal party. For some bridal parties, this just does not make sense. If you have a huge bridal party, and you can't all fit at a head table, then, you might want to stick to a sweetheart table. Or if you have a number of friends in your bridal party who have significant others who are not part of the bridal party, it makes it a bit awkward to either make the significant other sit somewhere else for the reception or add in all those extra people to the head table. Once again, these are just the little details that you need to think through as you are planning the wedding.

As you are making the decision about head table versus sweetheart table, you also need to begin thinking about seating assignments for your guests. It is imperative to take the time to create a seating chart. You and the groom are the only two people who will know everyone in the room. Everyone else may know some people, but they don't know everyone. I was at one wedding that did not provide a seating chart, and when it came time to sit down for the meal, it was a bit awkward as the group of us that all knew each other could not all fit at the same table. There were a few people who had to find a table elsewhere. They, of course, did not have as much fun because they were sitting with a bunch of people they did not know. Do your guests a favor and think through the seating arrangement and make a seating chart.

The day of the wedding, you will provide your guests with the seating chart and name cards with their table assignments. You can either provide just a table number or an escort card. Table numbers allow your guests to pick whichever seat they would like at the table. Escort cards are cards on the table indicating exactly which is your seat. You would find your table number on the seating chart and then go to the table to find your exact seat. Your table arrangements and guests assigned to each table will help indicate if you should provide your guests with just a table number or an escort card.

A few weddings I have been to have provided the escort cards because the tables were large, and they wanted to make sure that the people who knew each other were all seated together and not left sitting by people they do not know. I have found that at every wedding, there is always at least one table that is just kind of the "leftover" people. You are not sure where to seat these people, so you put them all together and hope they find something to talk about for the evening. Let me tell you; I have certainly been at one of these tables before. I have also been to two weddings where I was sitting at the same table as my ex-boyfriend. The first wedding where this happened, it had not been that long since we had broken up, and it was a bit awkward. The second time, it was years later, and it was great to be able to catch up.

Probably the worst situation I was at in regard to seating assignments was at a wedding where I was at a table of all friends from my hometown, and then, a random girl came up to our table and said she was supposed to be sitting at our table. There was not a chair or table setting for her, so we sent her away. A few minutes later, someone from the venue brought an extra chair and placed setting, and this girl joined our table.

Talk about awkward! I really felt sorry for the girl. We all knew each other, and she did not know anyone at the table and only knew a handful of people at the wedding altogether. She was a sweet young lady, but it really was an awkward situation, and we all felt bad that we sent her away. Later, I found out from the bride that she was a last-minute invite when one of the girls at our table was no longer bringing a plus one, but unfortunately, the updated information did not get passed along to the event coordinator.

To make matters worse, this poor girl got lost on her way to the ceremony and missed the whole ceremony and, then, was late to the reception and had nowhere to sit. I really felt sorry for her. Do your guests a favor and ensure every guest is accounted for, for the reception and don't leave anyone out. Think through your seating chart and do your best to ensure there are no awkward situations.

Finding the perfect wedding venue may seem like a daunting task at first, but once you begin making a plan for the number of guests, have an understanding of your guest's needs and—keeping your budget in mind—you will be able to find the wedding venue of your dreams. There are so many venues to choose from, and each one has their own unique atmosphere that you are guaranteed to find the right one for you!

Lessons:

- Have an estimated guest count before even beginning to look at venues.
- Select a venue with your guests in mind.
- Ask questions and know what your venue provides; is it a full-service or limited-service venue?
- Take time to make a seating chart and provide escort cards if needed.

Notes:

_____
_____
_____
_____
_____
_____
_____
_____
_____
_____
_____
_____
_____
_____
_____
_____
_____
_____
_____
_____
_____
_____
_____
_____
_____
_____
_____
_____
_____
_____

You Can't Rub Frosting on the Bride's Face

Well, wouldn't you know it, Adam ran toward the couple right after they cut the cake and nicely fed it to each other and grabbed a fist full and smeared the cake on Courtney's face. Oh, man! This did not exactly go over very well.

Cutting of the Cake

One of my favorite parts of a wedding reception is the ceremonial cutting of the cake. There is a tradition where the bride and groom cut a small slice of the cake and feed each other the first piece of the cake. Sometimes, the couple decides to nicely feed each other while, other times, they smash the cake in each other's face, making a mess.

For most of the weddings I have been to that have decided not to have a traditional wedding cake, the couple will still do a ceremonial "cutting of the cake" with a small cake but then not serve it and offer other dessert options instead, like pie or cookies. For me, I am not a fan of this. I am not a pie person, and there is something about traditional wedding cake that I really like. In my opinion, if you are not going to serve cake to your guests, then, there is no need to do a ceremonial cutting of the cake. If you want to have that tradition at your reception, then, either serve cake or just cut the pie and feed it to each other, but that is just my opinion.

Some couples are very nice to each other when they cut the cake and politely feed it to one another while others smash it on each other's faces. I can go either way on this and think it just depends on the couple and their personalities. I believe that it also depends on how fancy your reception is and who your guests are, but feeding each other or smashing the cake in each other's face is really up to you. One thing I would advise though is to know your partner well enough and discuss this beforehand. The last thing you want is to smash cake in the bride's face and start the marriage off with a fight.

* * * * *

We were all sitting around the table at Courtney's reception after the meal, laughing and carrying on. The event staff was getting ready for the couple to cut the cake.

Adam, one of the bride's friends at our table who is a real jokester, said, "I think I should run up there as they are feeding each other the cake and smash cake into Courtney's face!"

Now, we are all a few drinks in at this point, and everyone at the table agreed that it would be funny but a *terrible* idea.

Justin, Adam's good friend, laughed and said, "Adam, that would be hilarious but probably not the best idea on Courtney's wedding."

"Yeah, but think of all the laughs and what a great memory," Adam rebutted.

"You only live once. I am going to do it!" Adam exclaimed as he took another sip of his cocktail.

"Nooo!" Everyone from our table yelled as Adam went running for the bride and groom at the cake.

Well, wouldn't you know it, Adam ran toward the couple right after they cut the cake and nicely fed it to each other and grabbed a fist full and smeared the cake on Courtney's face. Oh, man! This did not exactly go over very well.

Courtney and her groom, Billy, were very intentional about not wanting to smash cake in each other's faces, due to the symbolism of respect. And here comes Adam, just attending the wedding, putting his hand in the cake, and smashing it into the bride's face. While the couple tried to play it off okay, Courtney was very upset, and for a second, I thought Billy was going to punch Adam out. The look on his face was pretty scary. But the scariest thing of all was how upset Courtney's mother was. If there is anything I have learned from all the weddings, it is never upset the mother of the bride. I don't know for sure, but I am pretty positive Adam immediately regretted this decision. But regardless, it makes a pretty good story and a fun memory for all.

On the wedding day, you have to respect the bride. While there may have been a lot of tension to get to this day, it is the couple's wedding day, and you must do whatever it takes to respect the bride. She is the prettiest woman you have ever seen, and everything about the wedding is perfect. You most certainly can't rub frosting in the bride's face. Only the groom can do that.

Wedding Desserts

Speaking of cake, I have seen a lot of different dessert options in the various weddings I have attended. Not every wedding had a traditional wedding cake. Being a bit of a dessert connoisseur, I tend to pay close attention to the dessert options. Of course, many people do have the traditional multilayer wedding cake with various flavors.

Typically, the bride and groom will do a cake tasting with the bakery and select their wedding cake flavor and design. I have seen some very extravagant wedding cakes with each layer being a different flavor of cake, icing, and filling. I have also seen some simpler wedding cakes that are still multilayered, but all the same flavor and icing throughout the cake. Some wedding cakes have very detailed designs and flowers while others are on the simpler side. It really is up to you on what you want your cake to look and taste like.

Another tradition is to have a bride and groom figurine on the top of the cake. This is something that is not as prevalent nowadays. Although, I have seen some unique cake toppers like penguins or Disney characters. Couples are taking an old tradition and making a modern twist to it.

For Elizabeth's wedding cake, she and her family wanted to be able to serve large pieces of cake to all their guests as well as give everyone the chance to try the different flavor of the cake. They ordered more cake than you typically would for the number of people attending the wedding. They encouraged people to have seconds. The cake was so good; I had a couple of pieces myself and, of course, tried all the different flavors. People certainly took advantage of the extra cake, and it was all gone by the end of the night. While not everyone is going to eat the cake, you need to make sure you have enough, so everyone who wants a slice gets some cake. I would be pretty upset if I attended a wedding and did not get a piece of the delicious wedding cake.

Another dessert option in addition to the regular wedding cake is to have a groom's cake. Groom's cakes are typically decorated in a manly fashion with something they enjoy on it. The groom's cakes I have seen are usually sheet cakes and provide an extra cake to be cut and served to the guests. Traditional wedding cakes are very expensive, so by having a groom's cake, you can purchase a smaller, traditional layered wedding cake and then still have enough cake for all your guests with the extra sheet cake.

If you are not interested in having a groom's cake but still want to find a cheaper alternative to providing enough cake for your guests, buy a sheet cake and just keep it in the back. You will have a smaller wedding cake and ask the event staff to cut both cakes to serve at the same time. Your guests will never notice the difference, and you can save a lot of money as well as offer two different flavors of cake and not spend a fortune. If you are on a budget and don't want to spend as much on your wedding cake, this is definitely something to consider.

When I was in Saudi Arabia for a wedding, the wedding cake was massive. As my friend and I walked to the dining room, the first thing you see is the cake. I literally stopped dead in my tracks, jaw dropped, and I said, "Is that thing real?" While the whole thing was not real, the section that was, was still a lot of cake. Besides the cake, they also had tables filled with other dessert options. This was certainly the largest cake/dessert display I had ever seen!

A new trend I have been seeing is to have cupcakes instead of a giant wedding cake or in addition to a smaller wedding cake. At Taren's wedding, they set the cupcakes up on tiers, so it looked like a wedding cake, but it was just cupcakes. Guests could then come up and grab a cupcake when they wanted after the dinner. They had a large cupcake that they did the traditional "cutting of the cake" but only served the cupcakes for the dessert.

Other things I have seen are cookies, pies, and chocolate fountains. I have also been to a few weddings where there was no cake at all served, just a bunch of different pies. The bride and groom were not cake people, so they chose to serve pie instead. It is your day, and you get to decide what type of dessert you want to serve. Just because wedding cake is "tradition" does not mean you have to do it. Make the day your own and enjoy your favorite dessert. At my wedding, if I ever get married, I plan on serving the cake first.

Keeping the Top Tier

It is a tradition that the top tier of the cake is to be saved for the bride and groom to freeze and eat on their first anniversary. While I have had a few friends who have done this, all of them said the cake was really not good a year later. Even though it did not taste very good and a bit freezer burnt, they ate some of it anyway because it is tradition and something fun for them to enjoy together. A newer trend I am seeing is that the bakery where the couple bought their wedding cake will make a small top tier cake a year later for the couple's one-year anniversary. This is something the bakery includes in the wedding cake package when the couple buys the cake. This is a much better way to go because you get fresh cake and not stale, frostbitten cake. Not every bakery will do this for you, but it does not hurt to ask during your cake tasting.

Serving the Cake

How the cake is served will depend on your wedding venue and the timing of the cake cutting. Some weddings, a slice of cake is served to each place setting even if people are up on the dance floor. You simply get whatever slice they put in front of you even if there are different flavors. Other weddings, I have seen a dessert station set up in the room, and people can just grab a slice of cake on their own time throughout out the reception. This allows the guests to pick their piece and only the guests who want dessert will get one.

If for some reason you do not have a large-enough cake to feed all your guests, I would suggest doing a dessert station with the cake slices and then maybe a few other dessert options. Not everyone is going to eat the cake, so even if your cake does not have enough slices, this option typically works out just fine. You can also do a sheet cake as I mentioned before to save a little money.

Whatever you decide to do in regard to dessert, make it your own and don't do something just because it is a tradition. This is your wedding day, and you can do whatever you want. If you don't like cake, then, don't waste your money on a cake. If you want a dessert bar with lots of options, then do that; if you like pie, serve pie. Your wedding really is your day, and you get to plan it however you want. Do not let others influence you on doing something out of tradition if that is not what you want to do.

Lessons:

- Only the groom can smash cake on the bride's face.
- Talk to your future husband or wife and make sure you both agree to smash the cake in each other's faces or feed it to each other nicely.
- While, traditionally, there is a wedding cake, it is up to you what type of dessert you would like to serve at your wedding.
- To save money, buy a smaller multitier cake and then a simple sheet cake kept in the back.
- Work with your bakery to get a fresh top tier cake made on your one-year anniversary.

Notes:

No One Remembers the Food

Little did we know that some tables were missing the main course and only had side dishes or vice versa. We figured those dishes were on their way. Well, we were wrong, and the caterers ran out of food.

Plated, Buffet, or Family Style

There are only a handful of weddings that I actually remember the food. Most wedding food is not very good or memorable. But what people do remember is if they had to wait in line at the bar. The majority of your guests want to enjoy the reception and partake in a few cocktails. If they have to wait a long time for a drink, the guests become annoyed. I don't know about you, but I have come to expect that wedding food is not going to be exquisite, so my expectations are low, but keep your guests happy by maintaining the bar lines. As you know, you have a few different options regarding your food—plated meal, buffet, action stations, or table family style.

Adriane's wedding was outside, and she had tables set out on different tiers of a hill. The number of people at each table varied to accommodate the setting. I was sitting with a bunch of Adriane's cousins. I did not know anyone, but I am pretty good at making conversation with anyone and had a great time. It was time for the meal to be served, and many people were still lingering by the bar or just hanging out, not sitting at their table. The servers started serving the meal, and it was set up family style.

Large dishes of food were placed in the center of the tables, and we were to serve ourselves and then pass the food dish around the table. One thing we did not realize was we were supposed to share the food dishes with the table next to us. Each table was served two to three food dishes and then meant to pass them to the next table to ensure everyone got all the items.

Well, we did not realize we were supposed to do that. Everyone assumed all tables had the same food and just started passing the dishes amongst ourselves and started eating. Little did we know that some tables were missing the main course and only had side dishes or vice versa. We figured those dishes were on their way. Well, we were wrong, and the caterers ran out of food. There was not enough food to go around since people did not realize the portions of the dish were for more than one table and took larger portions for themselves.

When the servers realized what had happened, they tried to go around to the tables and see which tables were missing what items and pass things along. At our table, there were a few people who got up to go to the bar and did not have any food on their plate yet, and the servers wanted to take the food away.

"Um, excuse me, where are you taking the salmon?" Judy said to the server.

"You are supposed to share the dishes with this table next to yours, so I am taking it to them, so they get some salmon as well," explained the server.

"Well, Jim, my husband, and Frank are up at the bar and have not gotten any food yet. Can I please serve them before you take the salmon away?" asked Judy.

"Of course," said the server, and she put a small piece of salmon on Jim and Frank's plates. It actually became quite comical as people were grabbing for food and trying to get as much on their plates before the servers took the dishes.

The servers did their best, but unfortunately, the concept was not explained very well, and it led to not everyone getting to enjoy all the food options. The good thing is no one left hungry. Everyone may not have been able to try everything, but everyone got fed. This family style meal seemed like a neat idea at first, but, it unfortunately was just not executed as well as it could have been.

One of my favorite buffet menus that I remember was at John's wedding. It was good old comfort food—barbecue, corn on the cob, and mashed potatoes. The reception was outside under a big tent on a beautiful, early fall day, and it was the perfect meal for the setting. It is always great when the caterers work with the bride and groom to provide a meal that is fitting for the venue and guests. This meal was perfect for this couple, and all the guests thoroughly enjoyed it. Barbecue is a simple meal and on the cheaper side, but because it was paired with great comfort food sides and the venue was outside making it a little more informal, it was perfect. On the flip side, if this was a plated meal at an upscale location, it would not have gone over quite as well.

One of my favorite plated meals was steak and potatoes. Michael and Sarah's wedding was on the swankier side, and they provided very high-end food. They had nice heavy hors d'oeuvre during the cocktail hour, and then soup, salad, main course, and dessert for the meal. Some of my friends at the wedding had not been to very many weddings or high-end weddings and did not understand that the hors d'oeuvres were just the appetizers. Then, when we were all seated, and they started serving the first course of crab soup, people thought this was the main dish.

"Does anyone want my crab soup? I don't like seafood," I said to my friends at my table.

"What! How do you live in Maryland and not like crab? I will eat it if you really don't want it," James said.

"I am not from Maryland, and I don't know, I just don't like any seafood," I replied.

"Hannah, I feel bad eating your dinner. Aren't you going to be hungry before the night is over?" James asked as I handed him my soup.

"Oh, this is just the first course, I am sure there will be other items throughout the evening that I will eat," I said.

"There is no way! The crab soup has to be the main course," everyone at the table exclaimed.

"No, I am pretty sure this is just the first course," I replied. Then, the salad came out, and everyone was shocked.

Before the main dish was served, we were all given sorbet to cleanse our pallet. I have only been to two weddings that had a pallet cleanser before bringing out the main dish. The pallet cleanser always makes me feel very fancy and reminds me of the movie *Princess Diaries*. After the pallet cleanser, we were served the main dish of steak and potatoes. This steak was so delicious; it was one of the best I have ever had. We all could not believe how much food there was, and it was all so good!

Michael and Sarah really wanted to provide that "wow" factor when it came to the food and chose to spend more money on food than other parts of their wedding. Everyone is a little different on what they feel is the top priority for their wedding. While this meal was indeed memorable, most wedding meals are not. If you and your fiancé are not big foodies, then, I would not stress too much about the food and spend more money on other parts of the reception.

Proper Wedding Etiquette

It amazes me how many wedding guests do not understand proper wedding etiquette when it comes to food. For a plated meal, if salads are preset on the table, then, it is acceptable for you to start eating your salad right away. When it comes to the entree, it is polite to wait for everyone at the table to be served before starting to eat your meal. This goes for buffets as well. Even though you are going through the buffet lines on your own, you are typically called to the buffet as a table, and it is best to wait for the entire table to sit back down with their food before starting to eat.

Table manners and etiquette matter, especially when you are at a formal occasion like a wedding. It always makes me laugh when I go to a wedding, and the salads and rolls are preset on the tables, and no one knows if they are supposed to eat them or not. You watch people look around and see what others are doing, and then, of course, you have one starved person who does not care and just dives in, and then someone else at the table that thinks you are supposed to wait. My advice is to eat the salad. Presetting the salads on the tables and having the guests start to eat right away helps with the timing of the food service from a catering/kitchen perspective.

Food and Beverage Cost

Food and beverages will be one of the most expensive parts of the wedding. While it sounds crazy, you will be shocked at how much this portion of the wedding costs. Most places charge per person, so one way to keep your costs down is to limit your guest list and keep your numbers low. If you are not willing to cut down your guest list, then, you will want to think of some creative ways to feed your guests.

A few things I have seen to cut down on the cost is to have a very limited cocktail-hour menu. While some people decide to spend the money and provide heavy hors d'oeuvres, you can keep this menu light and save some cash. Another thing that can add a cost is having passed hors d'oeuvres. When you need an attendant to pass hors d'oeuvres, there is typically an additional service fee. To avoid that extra cost, just have displayed food items.

Also, be very aware of what food items you are choosing for your cocktail hour. Since people are standing around and mingling, you want to make sure you are selecting items that are small, simple finger foods and not super messy. There is nothing worse than trying to enjoy a hors d'oeuvre, and it is messy with a dipping sauce, or you need more than one hand to eat it. I have certainly encountered those items, and you end up with sticky hands; it is just a mess. Most people will have a drink in one hand, so the food items need to be easy to handle and eat with only one hand.

I have seen some creative hors d'oeuvres like tomato soup in a shot glass with a small piece of grilled cheese on a toothpick on top and vegetable crudités in individual containers with the dressing at the bottom. Both of these items can be either passed or displayed and provide a neat twist on a traditional item that makes it easy to eat during a cocktail hour.

Other ways to save money on the food costs is to have a limited menu. There is a misconception that buffets are typically cheaper than a plated meal; this is not always the case. Due to the need to over-prepare and ensure everyone gets enough food, many times, buffets cost more than a plated meal. To help keep the cost down on a buffet, some caterers will choose to portion out and serve the food to help with consumption instead of making it a free for all. This way, you know you will have enough food, and the buffet does not run out before everyone gets through the line.

Before you sign on the dotted line and book your caterer, ensure they will *not* run out of food. There is nothing worse than the last few tables going through the buffet lines, and their portions are tiny or some items have run out. Caterers should know to over-prepare, so they don't run out, but ensure you discuss this with them when you are booking them for your wedding. Put a clause in the contract about running out of food to ensure this does not happen.

I have seen extensive buffets with three or four protein options, five sides, various salads, and more. This is great but certainly not necessary. You can provide an excellent meal and limit the options to a meat and vegetarian option with a simple salad, vegetable, and starch. The menu is really up to you, and I would not stress too much about it. Like I said before, most people don't remember the food.

While you want to make sure you are feeding your guests, I would rather spend money on other parts of the wedding and limit the food because I know when trying to feed a large group of people all at once, the food is never fabulous. Another thing I have seen to help keep costs down is to use paper products instead of china plates. While I am certainly not a big fan of this option, depending on your venue, caterer, and theme for the wedding, it can be pulled off and not seem too tacky.

Bar Packages

Spending a ton of money on food is not my focus, but putting that money toward the bar and alcohol package is a big deal. I do understand for some people they do not drink or alcohol is not a priority for them, and that is fine. But for the weddings I have been to, having a bar makes a big difference in the enjoyment of the day for your guests. If you are not a big drinker, you don't have to drink, but it is a good idea to still offer some type of cash bar or place in the venue for people to purchase alcohol if they would like.

If you are a drinker, then, I would always suggest an open bar. While I do understand this is the most expensive option, it is worth it for your guests. You can always do an open bar for cocktail hour and then a cash bar for the reception to save money if needed. There are a lot of different alcohol options, and you can purchase a less expensive package and offer an open bar and still save money.

I have seen it all when it comes to alcohol packages. Some couples go over the top and have multiple luxury bar options with top-shelf liquor and open bar all night. Other couples do a cash bar, making the guests pay for their alcohol, while others do a little bit of both with an open bar during the cocktail hour and cash bar during the reception.

* * * * *

Kathy's wedding was located at a campground, and she provided a basic red and white wine for the reception but encouraged the guests to "smuggle" in alcohol. Kathy did not want to spend a whole lot of money on alcohol and needed to abide by the venue's policies but wanted her guests to have a fantastic time so encouraged the guests to bring their own. I went to the wedding with some good friends who know how to have fun. Our table was filled with all sorts of liquor and mixers. Other guests were coming to us to enjoy a drink. Not every venue will allow this to take place, but for this wedding, it worked out well.

Another wedding where the couple wanted to keep costs down and were not huge drinkers did a very basic open bar with limited beer and wine option. They also did a champagne toast, and then, the leftover champagne was at the bar. Unfortunately, this bar seemed to be just a hodgepodge of different options every time I went to the bar. They only displayed two bottles of beer and one bottle of wine at a time. When that option ran out, they would display a different type. It was a little odd if I do say so myself. For this couple, the bar was not their focus, and they did not put a whole lot of money toward the alcohol.

* * * * *

Cindy's wedding was located at a winery, and during the cocktail hour, they offered a tour of the winery and wine tasting for the guests. The ceremony and reception were in the same room, so they needed all of the guests to leave the room while they flipped it to set for the reception. The winery tour and wine tasting provided something for the guests to do during this time and a unique twist to the cocktail hour. Since the wedding was at a winery, they only offered wine served tableside during the dinner. There was no bar at this reception, and after dinner was over, the wine was taken away.

* * * * *

One thing I always like when it comes the alcohol package is when the couple has a signature drink and creates a cute name for it at the bar. I just love when couples bring in their personal touch and add something unique to each area of the wedding. Providing a signature drink typically does not cost a whole lot more but offers a little pizzazz to the bar. This is another one of those simple special touches that makes your guests feel like you thought of everything.

One thing to keep in mind with your food and alcohol package costs are the service fees and taxes. Many times, the price prepared by the venue or caterer does not include the service charge and tax upfront. These extra fees can be additional thousands of dollars that you did not budget for. Ensure that you discuss all extra service fees and taxes before you sign a contract and know exactly how much you will be paying for the selected packages.

Brunch, Lunch, or Dinner

Another thing to consider when choosing your meal and alcohol package is the time of day. I have been to weddings in the morning, afternoon, and evening. One of my friends loves breakfast food, so she chose to have a morning wedding and then do brunch with French toast, pancakes, bacon, and more for the reception. Obviously, for an early-morning wedding, having an open bar with full cocktails, beer, and wine may not be appropriate, but you can provide mimosas and Bloody Marys.

If you are having an afternoon wedding and doing more of a late lunch early dinner meal, then, it can be a lighter fare than a traditional evening wedding with a large formal dinner. The thing to keep in mind though is to try and have your reception line up with a mealtime or ensure your guests are fully aware of the timing of everything. There is nothing worse than having an afternoon wedding than three to four hours between the ceremony and reception and not eat dinner until really late. Your guests will be famished by the time dinner comes around. Work with your wedding planner or the onsite event coordinator to ensure the timing of everything makes sense, and there are not hours in between or hangry guests because they were not fed on time.

Another thing you will want to work with your wedding planner or event coordinator is ensuring the bride and groom get fed. Too often, the bride and groom are so preoccupied with visiting with all their guests that they don't get a chance to eat. Make a plan and ensure you get to eat the food that you spent so much time and money on. The food will be one of the most expensive meals you ever have, so be sure to enjoy it. Also, if you have a good bridal party, they will make sure you always have a drink in your hand and have a good time. If you need to, assign one of your girls to watch out for you and make sure you are taken care of, but don't overdo it and end up puking on your wedding night.

The ultimate goal is to ensure you and your guests have a fabulous time at the wedding! Don't overdo it so you don't remember the night, but have fun, let loose, and enjoy the day. The day will go by fast, and you will feel like you spent months planning for something that flew by, so don't get caught up in the details and just enjoy the day.

Lessons:

- Make sure everyone gets fed.
- Pay attention to the timing of events.
- Food will be expensive, but make sure your food options match your theme and venue.
- Focus more on alcohol packages than meal packages. No one remembers the food but will remember standing in long lines at the bar.
- Add special touches to each area of the reception such as a signature drink at the bar.

Notes:

_____

_____

_____

_____

_____

_____

_____

_____

_____

_____

_____

_____

_____

_____

_____

_____

_____

_____

_____

_____

_____

_____

_____

_____

_____

_____

_____

_____

_____

Don't Forget Your Pants

Don't let the father of the bride forget his pants;
maybe that is why priest wear robes.

Before You Leave for the Wedding,
Ensure You Have Everything

It is the morning of the wedding, and Cecelia's parents, Sue and James, are in their bed-and-breakfast room, getting ready. They had a relaxed morning, eating breakfast on the patio, reminiscing about their baby girl, and so excited for her to be marrying the love of her life. James will be officiating the wedding, so he is a little nervous and reviews his notes as Sue begins the get ready.

James starts to gather his clothing, as time is getting closer for them to meet at the venue for pictures.

James yelled to Sue, "Where are my pants?"

Sue replied, "Honey, they should be in your garment bag with your suit jacket and shirt."

"I don't see them in there," James replied.

"Well, look in our suitcase then, did you bring them?" Sue asked.

"Of course, I brought my pants," James replied. "Why would I forget my pants?"

"I don't know why you can't find them," said Sue.

At this point, Sue is starting to get annoyed at James, and James is starting to panic. He began rifling through the suitcase and garment bags, throwing clothes everywhere.

Sue comes out of the bathroom, dressed and ready to go, and sees James making a complete mess and begins to yell, "JAMES! WHAT ARE YOU DOING?"

James replied, "I told you I can't find my pants."

Sue is now very frustrated. "James, I just don't understand how you can't find your pants. Are you sure you packed them?"

"Of course, I packed my pants, how stupid do you think I am," replied James.

"I don't know, you are the one panicking, throwing clothes all over the room and can't find your pants for your daughter's wedding," replied Sue.

Finally, James takes a deep breath, sits on the bed, and remembers that he took his pants to the cleaners to be pressed last week. "Sue, did you pick up my pants from the cleaners?" asked James.

"No," replied Sue. "When did you take your pants to the cleaners?"

"I dropped them off last week," James said, feeling very embarrassed. "What am I going to do now? What am I going to wear to the wedding?" James is really starting to freak out now. "I not only have to walk our daughter down the aisle this afternoon, but I also have to stand up in front of everyone and officiate the wedding," said James.

Sue replied, "I guess you will have to wear a different pair of pants to the wedding."

"Sue, I don't have any pants with me, you know me, I wear shorts everywhere," James said.

"Well, I guess you are wearing shorts then," said Sue with a frustrated look on her face.

"Oh, man, I guess you are right, let's not tell Cecilia until we absolutely have to. I don't want to get her upset. There is nothing we can do about it at this point, so I don't want to get her worked up," said James.

Sue and James finished getting ready and headed to the venue to take some pictures prior to the ceremony. They run into the groom, Danny's, parents first. James starts to tell them about his pants, and Danny's mom, Pam, said, "Well, what are you going to do about it?"

James responded, pointing to his bright blue shorts, "I have already done it."

Pam was not impressed but, trying to be polite, simply said, "Okay," and did not make a big deal out of the situation.

It was time for Sue and James to get some pictures taken with Cecelia, and the truth would have to be shared. Sue walked into the bridal suite first and said, "Cecilia, don't get upset, but your father had some issues with his suit."

"What do you mean he has had some issues?" Cecilia questioned.

"Well, he forgot to pick up his pants from the cleaners and is wearing shorts," replied Sue.

While Cecelia was not too upset about this, the emotions of the day started to hit her, and she got upset for a minute and then took a deep breath and realized it really was no big deal. Cecilia knew that her father wears shorts ninety percent of the time and felt like this went right along with his personality. She was not about to let this ruin her day. She began laughing and called her dad into the bridal suite. Cecilia's attitude toward this situation and just going with the flow made a huge difference in the situation.

If Cecilia would have gotten really worked up and upset, it would have been a huge problem, but she did not let it ruin the day, and it became something for people to laugh at and enjoy the day. The photographer also did a great job of trying to take pictures of him from the waist up so that no one could tell years later in the photos.

While the photographer did a great job of trying to get pictures of him from the waist up, social media tells a different story. Friends and family members took lots of pictures and, of course, posted them on social media. Everyone got a good laugh out of this situation. We still talk about the father of the bride forgetting his pants to this day.

Understanding that things will go wrong on your wedding day and being okay with it makes all the difference. It is best to have a plan *B* and be prepared to just go with the flow. Life is filled with unpredictability, and how you handle the unpredictable mishaps makes a world of a difference in how much you enjoy the day.

Guests can sense the emotions and mood for the wedding from the bride and groom. If they get a sense that the bride and groom are nervous or upset, it can set the tone for the whole day. Having a negative tone looming over the wedding can really hinder how much fun you and your guests have at the wedding.

Handling the Unpredictability

Speaking of unpredictability, at Ashley's wedding, it was all planned and ready to be an outside ceremony and had to be moved indoors due to a torrential downpour. It was a summer wedding on a farm, and Ashley thought she had it all planned perfectly. The ceremony would be outside, overlooking the field and the reception inside the gorgeous old barn. She had beautiful decorations and lighting to make it pop and was so excited for the big day. While Ashley knew there was a chance it could rain on her wedding day, she planned the ceremony outside and hoped for the best.

If you want an outdoor wedding, have a backup plan in case of inclement weather. A few options for a plan *B*, if the weather does not cooperate, would be to have a tent setup and move everything inside the tent. Many venues will have an inside space to reserve for inclement weather. There might be an additional cost to reserve both the outside and backup inside area, but if there is inclement weather, it will be worth it. If the weather is just colder than expected, you could always provide some heaters outside to keep your guests warm and, of course, encourage them to get on the dance floor. That is a sure fire way to warm anyone up. Having a plan *B* is imperative when planning an outside wedding.

For Ashley, unfortunately, as luck would have it, it not only rained; it poured. People say it is good luck to have it rain on your wedding day, and I guess, for Ashley, seven years and three kids later, she has been pretty lucky. The day of the wedding, it rained almost the entire day, so early in the day, they decided to move the ceremony into the barn. A few tables were rearranged to make an easy path for the bride to walk down the "aisle," and the ceremony took place right in the center of the barn on the dance floor. As people arrived, they were directed to get their escort card and sit at their table assignment for the reception.

While this was not an ideal situation, the couple made the most of it and did not let a little rain get in their way. They had a plan B and moved forward with the day. They provided the ushers with large umbrellas to help escort people from their cars to the barn and fully enjoyed their wedding day despite a "little" rain. While it was not intentional for the guests to sit at their reception table for the ceremony at this wedding, I have seen this concept at other weddings.

When the ceremony and reception are all in the same room and instead of having the venue staff flip the room and make everyone leave the room for an hour, they simply had everyone sit at their assigned tables for the ceremony and reception. It works out quite nicely and makes for a one-stop shop for the guests. The only downside of this concept is the guests stay in the same place for a long time. It can make the "cocktail hour" seem a bit longer since there is not a whole lot of movement, and people don't have anything to do during this time since they are already at their tables for dinner.

Back to Ashley's barn wedding; the best part of this wedding needing to be moved inside the barn was the perfect timing of the rain. It poured pretty much the whole day except for the few minutes Ashley needed to walk from the house to the barn. The rain let up, and she was able to walk to the ceremony without ruining her hair or dress. Of course, she had a whole entourage helping her hold up her dress, so it did not drag in the mud. Then, as the ushers opened the barn doors, oh my gosh, Ashley was standing there with the sun beaming behind her. It was like a moment taken out of a movie.

Ashley was absolutely stunning, and it was so fantastic how perfectly the timing of the rain let up. Ashley certainly did not expect it to rain that day. She planned and hoped it would not, but when it did, she had a plan *B* to ensure her day was not ruined. And then, when it came time for her big entrance, it could not have been any better. A ray of sunshine on a gloomy day to start her marriage off right.

No matter how well you plan the day, there will be things that go wrong or you will realize you forgot something. Take a deep breath, remember we are all human, and everything will be okay. Be prepared with a plan *B* for the big stuff and expect little things to pop up along the way.

As you are doing the planning for the big day, know that things will go wrong. Someone might forget their pants, or it may rain so hard you have to make modifications to the ceremony or reception. Have a backup plan for the big things and be okay when the little things happen. Walk through every aspect of the ceremony and reception and ensure that you have everything covered and don't need any extra people to help execute your perfect wedding day. Then, take a deep breath, relax, and enjoy the day.

Lessons:

- If someone forgets their pants, don't let it ruin the day, but laugh and move on.
- Always have a plan *B* in case it rains or some other major mishap happens, so it does not ruin the day.
- Don't forget the last-minute details; keep a checklist to ensure everything is covered.

Notes:

_____
_____
_____
_____
_____
_____
_____
_____
_____
_____
_____
_____
_____
_____
_____
_____
_____
_____
_____
_____
_____
_____
_____
_____
_____
_____
_____
_____
_____
_____
_____

Boom Boom Sauce
(The Special Touch)

I have heard over and over again from most brides and grooms that they did not get a chance to eat at their wedding. They do all this planning, food tasting, and then, when it comes time to eat, they are too busy trying to visit with each guest that they don't get to enjoy their meal. Because of this, most brides are starving by the time they get to their hotel room for the night. This is where the Boom Boom Sauce comes in.

Making Your Wedding Unique

The special touches that the bride and groom provide for the wedding are really what make the wedding special and unique. Each couple brings their personality to their wedding. Some of the neat things I have seen are fire pits, cornhole, a string quartet for the ceremony, glow sticks on the dance floor, and baskets in the bathroom with all the necessities. Having a cute little basket in the bathroom with lotion, mouthwash, and feminine products are a nice touch that lets your guests think you thought of everything. Most venue bathrooms are not super nice, so this adds a little bit of class to a bathroom.

Scott's wedding provided cornhole at the reception. He knew they had many guests who were not into dancing and would not enjoy the DJ and dancing part of the reception. They decided to have an area to play cornhole and have a bonfire. Guests that did not want to dance enjoyed having alternative options of things to do, and many guests stayed until the very end of the reception. This was the second time I had seen a fire pit at a wedding reception.

The first time I saw a fire pit at a wedding was at Elizabeth and Samuel's wedding. Their wedding ceremony was outside at a vineyard, and the reception inside the barrel room. Elizabeth and Samuel knew that some people might want to hangout outside on the patio but knew it would be a little chilly outside, so they provided a few small fire pits and all the fixings for s'mores. This was an excellent little-added bonus dessert option as a late-night snack toward the end of the reception.

Another favorite add-on I have seen at a number of weddings is providing pairs of flip-flops for the ladies to wear on the dance floor. We all know that women enjoy wearing high heels when they get all dressed up, but when it comes to dancing, high heels are the worst. Stock up on cheap flip-flops, put a cute bow around them, and voila, you have a little special touch to encourage dancing, and your guests will thank you. All of these special extra touches provide a unique flair to the wedding.

To go along with the flip-flops to encourage people to get on the dance floor, I have seen glow sticks provided. Some weddings, this is provided by the DJ; others, the bride and groom bring them; and one wedding, I even saw one of the guests bring the glow sticks. The bride was not particularly excited this guest brought the glow sticks, but she just rolled with it and did not make a fuss.

Glow sticks can add a little excitement to the reception and get people motivated to dance. At Brittany's wedding, the DJ brought a whole bunch of glow sticks, glow glasses, and noisemakers. This DJ did it up and got a lot of people on the dance floor with the props.

It added a fun element to the reception. Those who were dancing entertained the people who did not want to dance.

The special touch that stands out to me the most from a ceremony is a string quartet. I simply just loved that the couple decided to have a string quartet provide the music for the ceremony. While they did have a DJ for the reception, this was a very elegant special touch for the ceremony.

Momzilla

We have all heard of the term "bridezilla," when the bride is super demanding and almost a bit unrealistic with their expectations during the planning process of the wedding. But have you heard of "momzilla?" Momzilla is the mother of the bride who is just as much, if not more, insane than the bride. Unfortunately, weddings can bring out the worst in people and turn moms into a momzilla.

One mother-daughter duo had multiple major fights while planning the daughter's wedding. Elizabeth wanted a small wedding while her mom, Sue, wanted to invite the whole town. Throughout the planning process, Elizabeth and Sue clashed on almost everything. They battled things out for the months leading up to the wedding. It got to the point where Sue would just do things without even asking Elizabeth. Talk about a "momzilla."

After numerous fights, one day, Sue called Elizabeth. "I have a fantastic idea for the wedding!" Sue exclaimed.

"What is it now, Mom?" Elizabeth questioned.

"I was out shopping, and I found these beautiful pashminas. I think we should buy a bunch and have them available for the ladies at the wedding," Sue explained.

"Mom, we have already gone way over budget, and I don't think that is necessary," Elizabeth argued.

"Elizabeth, don't worry about the budget. The wedding is outside, and the ladies might get cold when the sun goes down," Sue rebutted.

"Mom, it is not going to be cold, the ladies will be fine. It is not our job to provide clothing for the guests if they don't dress appropriately for the wedding. This is my wedding, and I don't think it is necessary," Elizabeth argued back. After a few minutes of silence, they both just hung up the phone.

Well, Sue went ahead and ordered the pashminas and shipped them to Elizabeth's house the week of the wedding without her even knowing. By the time the big day rolled around, Elizabeth was so sick of arguing about every little detail that she put the pashminas in a lovely basket and brought them to the wedding. To her surprise, the pashminas were a big hit. It ended up being a chilly evening once the sun went down, and all the ladies enjoyed the pashminas and still talk about it to this day. Moral of this story, "Mother always knows best."

Bridal Survival Kit

One of the best things I have seen that I believe is an absolute must-have is the survival kit for the bridal party. The bridesmaids should create a small kit to take with them everywhere during the wedding day. This kit can have items such as stain remover sticks, bobby pins, hairspray, sewing kit, deodorant, mints, feminine products, and any other small knickknack items you think you might need to ensure the day is flawless. You may not think this is necessary, but when the bridal party bus air conditioning breaks and birds poop on your dress while taking pictures, you are going to be glad there is deodorant and a stain remover stick close by.

Reception Styles

In the thirty-plus weddings I have been invited to, I have seen a few different reception styles. The majority of the receptions provide a standard cocktail hour, meal, and then dancing, but on occasion, I have seen a few different features. I have been to weddings in the morning that decided to do a mimosa cocktail hour and then brunch food for the meal. I have seen couples that were not into dancing, so they chose to do just a dessert bar and receiving line instead of a traditional reception. People hung around for a little while and said congratulations to the bride and groom, ate some dessert, and then went on their way. For this wedding, the ceremony was the primary focus.

While your wedding day is yours, and you can set up the wedding however you would like, you should be mindful of your guests. Ensure your guests are informed about what type of ceremony/reception there will be and be sensitive to guests who are traveling for the day. Nowadays, so many people are traveling to attend your wedding, and it would be quite disappointing if they traveled hours to see you get married and then did not realize there was no traditional reception and left hungry and angry. No one wants hangry guests.

Another neat idea I have seen for a reception when you have a lot of people you want to invite to your wedding but also want a more intimate reception is to do two different receptions. Marcie had an enormous ceremony and invited everyone to the mini reception at the church right after the ceremony with light fare and then a private, invitation-only full reception with dinner.

This allowed the couple to invite as many guests as they wanted to the ceremony but keep costs down and only have close friends and family at the full reception. The mini reception right after the ceremony was more like a cocktail hour, but since it was at a church, there were no cocktails. All the guests who attended the ceremony had the opportunity to give their well-wishes to Marcie and her husband, but then, the real close friends and family attended the full dinner and dancing reception which took place at a different venue later in the evening.

Couple Send-Off and After-Party

Traditionally, at the end of the wedding, before the bride and groom leave, they will have some type of send-off. I have seen a few different send-offs for couples when they exit the reception, and none of them excites me. The most common thing I have seen is a sparkler send off. All the guests get a sparkler to hold and line up on either side, and the bride and groom run through on their way out the door.

If you decide to do a send-off where your guests have to go outside, make sure you consider the weather. I was at one wedding where they did a sparkler send-off in the middle of February in Pennsylvania. Man, was it cold. Everyone bundled up, trekked outside, grabbed a sparkler, and lined up. We were outside for quite a while before the couple came running through the sparklers.

What made things even worse with this one was the fact that this was just a photo opportunity, and the couple was not actually leaving. They ran through, got a bunch of pictures, and then, everyone including the bride and groom came back inside to finish out the reception. While I understand couples have ideas of what they want and what kind of pictures they want to capture for their special day, but this broke up the flow of the reception. Not to mention, it was not very considerate of their guests considering it was so cold.

Other things I have seen with the couple send-offs are decorating the car. This is a very old tradition, and some people love it while others hate it. I have been to weddings where the couple expects the bridal party to decorate the car and loves being able to drive away in a decorated car after the reception. I have also seen other couples purposely hide their car, so it cannot be decorated because they do not want anything to do with that. It is important to know what the couple wants, so there are no surprises, and people don't get upset that you did or did not decorate the car.

Although, some of my favorite weddings have been when the bride and groom don't have a send-off at all but stay until the very end of the wedding and then join the guests for an after-party. Most of the time, the after-party is not planned before the evening, but a bunch of the guests don't want the fun to end, so they gather up as many attendees as possible and head to a local bar or club to continue with the fun. Sometimes, the bride and groom are up for it while other times, they are ready to go back to their hotel room and be husband and wife.

When determining if you want to have a special send-off at the end of the wedding, think through the logistics of the evening and decide if it is worth it or not for you. If you are expecting guests to stand outside in the freezing cold, or rain, or scorching hot sun, it may not be the picture-perfect idea you are thinking.

Also, think about the time of day when the reception is supposed to wrap up and the send-off take place. If you have a Sunday afternoon wedding or a really late evening reception, there is a good chance many of your guests will leave early especially if they had to travel far to attend. Doing a send-off once the majority of the guests have gone does not quite have the same effect.

Late-Night Snack

I have heard over and over again from most brides and grooms that they did not get a chance to eat at their wedding. They do all this planning, food tasting, and then, when it comes time to eat, they are too busy trying to visit with each guest that they don't actually get to enjoy their meal. Because of this, most brides are starving by the time they get to their hotel room for the night. This is where the Boom Boom Sauce comes in.

Madison was starving by the time the ceremony and reception were over. She and her new husband were in their hotel room when I got a text, "Hannah, I am starving! Can you please bring me some food?"

Well, a few of us loaded up in my car and headed to Sheetz. If you are unfamiliar with Sheetz, it is a gas station, convenience store, and fast-food place all rolled into one. In our small little town where I grew up, this was the hangout spot, and the perfect place for a late-night snack.

So there we were, five of us all dressed up, most a little drunk, placing made-to-order (MTO) food at Sheetz. I did my best to keep everyone under control so we don't get kicked out, and then, we found the Boom Boom Sauce.

"Guys, guys, guys! Look at this, *Boom Boom* Sauce," Felecia exclaimed.

Everyone ran over to Felecia and just started laughing. "What is Boom Boom Sauce," Eric asked.

"I don't know, but I think we all need some," said Felecia.

"Let's get some for Madison also!" Kristy chimes in.

Of course, we all needed the Boom Boom Sauce and got some for Madison as well. At midnight and after having a few drinks, Boom Boom Sauce sounds much funnier than it does as I am typing this. I guess you had to be there.

We delivered the food to the bridal suite to find out that the groom is passed out on the bed, and Madison was up, waiting for her food. We all hung out in the parlor area of the hotel suite, eating our food and chatting for a while before I drove everyone home for the evening. While this was not the ideal wedding night the bride envisioned, it certainly is a great memory. The moral of the story is to make sure the bridal suite is fully stocked with food before the wedding, so the bride does not starve for the night, and you are not out, ordering fast food at midnight.

I have heard that some venues are now starting to prepare two extra meals toward the end of the reception and send them to the couple's room after the event since they know they don't get a chance to eat with everyone else. This is something you would certainly have to work out with your venue and event manager, but something to think about if you are staying at the same place as the reception.

The wedding is all about you, and you get to decide what you want and how you want it to be set up. There are no right or wrong ways to plan your wedding, but adding your special touches to the wedding will make a big difference. When you add your special touches, it makes your guests feel like you thought of everything and can add that extra, unique twist to your special day. Since most weddings are similar, it is the extra pizzazz that stands out to people.

Lessons:

- The extra-special, unique touches make a big difference.
- Spend the money and time adding the extra special touches for the ceremony and reception.
- Don't forget the bridal party survival kit.
- Make sure the bride and groom eat and stock their hotel room with food for after the wedding.
- The wedding is your day, so do things the way you want; there is no right or wrong way to plan your wedding.

Notes:

Traditions

Something old, something new, something borrowed,
something blue, a sixpence in your shoe.

While there are so many wedding traditions, times have changed, and there are no longer set rules for a wedding anymore. You can do whatever you like. The wedding is your day, so plan it the way you want and don't worry about what anyone thinks!

Traditionally, the bride's family pays for the wedding, and the groom's family pays for the rehearsal dinner. As many couples are getting married later in life and both working full-time, I am finding that, many times, the couples will pay for the majority of the wedding themselves, and then, both families will also contribute and pay for a portion of the wedding to help supplement.

The Budget

Times have changed, and there are no set standards of who needs to pay for what anymore. The most significant thing you need to do is to set a budget and work within your budget during the planning process. Decide what a reasonable dollar amount you and your fiancé want to invest into your wedding day. According to theknot. com, "The average wedding cost is $33,931" (*Wedding Budget 101*). Without setting a budget, the planning goes crazy, and before you know it, your wedding has turned into a three-ring circus.

One evening I received a call from my friend, Dan, a few days after he got engaged, and he asked my opinion if I could tell the difference between a twenty-thousand-dollar and a fifty-thousand-dollar wedding. While I do think for many weddings, you can tell if the bride and groom had a higher budget or not; when it comes down to it, the dollar amount should not matter. I have been to extremely expensive, outrageous weddings that were not as much fun and have been to weddings that were very budget conscience and had a blast. Things I have found that make a difference are the guests that attend and your connection to the bride and groom.

Weddings where a lot of my friends attended and I am very close to the bride and groom are a lot more fun, no matter how much the bride and groom spent on the wedding. You have to remember this is only one day, and it is a good idea to set a reasonable budget for the day and not go into debt for your wedding. Once you have decided on a budget, it is a lot easier to make the rest of the decisions needed in the planning process. Although, there are some decisions that you need to make that have nothing to do with money but merely tradition.

Something Old

Have you heard the saying, "Something old, something new, something borrowed, something blue, a sixpence in your shoe?" These are five little good-luck charms for the big day. The bride can carry them or add them to her wedding dress. Typically, the bride's close friends and family members give these five items to her the day of the wedding. The something old represents community, and the something new represents optimism for the future. The something borrowed symbolizes borrowed happiness, and the something blue stands for purity and love. The sixpence in your shoe is typically a British tradition, but it represents a wish for good fortune and prosperity (Wedding Traditions). I know of two friends who added this tradition to their wedding day.

Timing of Photographs

Another old tradition is the idea of the groom not seeing the bride in her wedding dress before the ceremony. Many couples have done away with this tradition and tend to use the time before the ceremony to take some pictures. They do a "first look" photo shoot, where the groom sees the bride for the first time in her dress.

While there are pros and cons for doing pictures before the ceremony, I prefer pictures after the ceremony, but that is just my preference. I love when the groom has not seen the bride before the ceremony, and I enjoy watching his face when she walks down the aisle. I love seeing the groom get emotional when seeing his bride for the first time.

I do understand that for some couples, depending on how they have set up their day, they prefer to take pictures before the ceremony to save time and get to fully enjoy the cocktail hour and reception, but I like it when they wait. Although, if the couple wants to take a *lot* of pictures, and it is going to take too much time, it might be best to take them before the ceremony. This way, the couple does not miss out on the entire reception or have too much time in between the ceremony and cocktail hour.

At Cindy's wedding, she and Greg missed almost the whole dancing portion of the reception because they were off, taking pictures. They were big into photography and said the lighting was perfect outside during the reception. I don't know about you, but I don't want to miss out on the fun of the reception for pictures. I can take pictures anytime, but all my friends and family will only be gathered this one day, so I don't want to miss out on all the fun.

Reception Traditions

A few other traditions I have seen at the reception are the cutting of the cake, bouquet/guarder toss, and the apron dance. The wedding cake is not like any ordinary cake, and couples spend a lot of time picking the right cake for their perfect day. As mentioned earlier, there is the tradition of the bride and groom cutting the cake in front of everyone and feeding a small piece to each other. The couple will either romantically feed each other or decide to smash the cake in each other's faces. Either way is up to you, but you better know what the bride wants. Otherwise, you might be starting your marriage off on the wrong foot.

The bouquet-and-guarder toss is a tradition from a long time ago that is still prevalent in many weddings to this day. The bride gathers all of the single women on the dance floor and turns around and then tosses a bouquet of flowers in hopes that one lucky single lady will catch it. Let me tell you, I have been to some weddings where no one wanted to admit they are single or catch the bouquet, and it dropped to the ground. I have also been to other weddings that it became a bit of a "cat fight" between the ladies. The single women leapt for the bouquet, and two people caught it at the same time.

After one lucky lady has been declared the winner, the bride and groom come to the center of the dance floor, and the bride sits down on a chair, and the groom is supposed to find her garter and pull it off. There have been some weddings where the groom is very appropriate and directly reaches his hands under the bride's dress and gets the garter. I have also seen other weddings where—OMG—I blushed with how sexual the groom was and how much time he spent under the bride's dress. It is always a little awkward when the groom takes things a bit too far sexually when retrieving the garter. Remember, your parents, the bride's parents, and most likely, grandparents are in the room, not to mention all your closest friends and possibly some coworkers. No one needs to have sexual images of the bride and groom in their head.

Once the garter has been retrieved, all the single men come to the dance floor, and the groom tosses the garter in hopes one lucky guy catches it. Depending on who caught the bouquet typically indicates how much of a fight the garter toss will be. Because, next, the woman who caught the bouquet sits down on a chair in the middle of the dance floor, and the man who caught the garter has to put it on the woman. Once again, this can get a little awkward. I have been to some weddings where it ended up being a couple who was just dating, and they both caught the items, and it was not that bad, but I have also seen when it was two random people having to get a little closer than most would find comfortable.

Tradition says that the man and woman who catch the bouquet and garter are the ones that will be getting married next. I have yet to see that come true, but it is a fun tradition and certainly adds some laughs to the reception.

Another fun tradition is the apron dance. I have only seen this a handful of times, but the idea behind the apron dance is you have to pay money to dance with the bride. Someone stands on the corner of the dance floor with an apron on and collects money, and then, you get in line to dance with the bride. Unfortunately, I have never seen this go over very well. Most people are not interested in dancing with the bride like they may have been years ago, not to mention who wants to pay to dance with the bride when you can dance with her for free every other song at the reception.

International Weddings

I was fortunate enough to be able to attend a wedding in Saudi Arabia and crashed a wedding in Egypt. Being able to experience weddings in different cultures is amazing. The wedding in Saudi Arabia was so different than any wedding I had been to in America. This opened my eyes to learning about different cultures and their traditions.

In Saudi Arabia, they have two different weddings. A groom's wedding for the men and a bride's wedding for the women. Due to the laws and regulations in Saudi Arabia, men and women don't typically socialize together, and women need to cover their hair in the presence of men outside their family. On Saturday, the women of the bride's family got together for a large traditional meal. There were about twenty of us including all the cousins, aunts, mother, and grandmother of the bride. During this same time, all the men gathered together for a traditional celebration meal with the groom's closest friends and family. The groom's wedding is much smaller than the brides. The men all go to dinner and then enjoy each other's company and socialize for a while. The women's wedding, on the other hand, oh my gosh, it is extravagant. I have never seen a wedding this elaborate.

The wedding had about three hundred guests which was considered a small wedding for Saudi Arabia. The room was set up with couches and coffee tables all around the perimeter of the room and a long walkway aisle down the center. The front of the room had a stage with a couch in the middle and a wall of flowers as the backdrop. The wedding did not start until about 9:30 p.m. The close family stood by the doorway to welcome the guests as they arrived. People arrived between 9:30 p.m. to 11:30 p.m., and then, at midnight, it was time for the "ceremony."

As people were arriving, I sat on the couches and watched as my friend, Leilah, and her family welcomed the guests. I met a lot of people, and many came up to me, saying, "Oh, you are Hannah from Snapchat, we have heard a lot about you." Leilah loved to use Snapchat, and little did I know she was snapping everything I did when I was in Saudi and told all her followers I would be attending the wedding.

As people were arriving, all the guests visited with each other and coffee, tea, water, chocolates, and savory treats were continually passed around for hours. I, of course, tried just about everything. Throughout the evening, I drank way more coffee than anyone should be ever allowed. I am not a coffee drinker, but the coffee in Saudi was fantastic. I also did not know how to tell the servers to stop pouring me more coffee, and every time I tried to give the cup back, they would pour me more coffee.

Then, at midnight, the "ceremony" began. Hijabs (scarves) were given out to the women who wanted to cover. Most of the women covered their hair, but many of the younger women did not. Then, the music started, and the men entered into the room.

The music was projected onto two large screens, and the band, which was all men, was in a different room, playing. I learned that if it were an all-women's band, then, they would be playing in the room, but since it was men, they cannot be in the same room. After the men walked in, which included the groom, the father of the bride, brothers of the bride, and uncles of the bride, then, the bride walked in. None of the men of the groom's family participated in the women's wedding. The bride was the most beautiful bride I had ever seen. I had never seen a wedding dress that gorgeous! She was absolutely stunning. The music played, and she slowly walked to the groom. When she got there, she kissed the groom on the cheek and the other men. They then took a lot of pictures, and everyone just watched and admired the beauty. After the pictures were finished, all of the men except for the groom left the wedding. The groom stayed with the bride for a little while, and then, he left as well. At that point, the dancing began.

I found it interesting that the bride came to the wedding in the middle of the evening and not at the beginning. The bride then sat at the front of the room all night, and people came up to take pictures and say hi to her all night long, but she never left her post at the front of the room. Weddings in Saudi Arabia are not about the bride at all; they are more about the guests and the display of the bride. The bride does not get to dance and enjoy the wedding or eat the food; she is just on display for all her guests.

All throughout the night, the band would play songs, and the guests would dance. Leilah taught me the traditional Saudi dance they do at weddings so I would get up and dance and enjoyed the festivities as well. It was so much fun. Leilah's family liked when I would dance and pulled me on the dance floor a few times. I think they liked seeing the American do their traditional dance, but I believe that they also were making fun of me a bit. Leilah promises they said I was a good dancer, and it was all positive, but they spoke in Arabic, so I could not understand, so I am not totally convinced. ☺

One of the differences between an American wedding and a Saudi Arabian wedding is how dressed up everyone gets for the wedding. While it is tradition in America that the bride and bridal party are very formal and will get their hair and makeup done, in Saudi Arabia everyone gets super dressed up with ball gowns, hair, and makeup. I could not believe how beautiful everyone was at the wedding. But the biggest thing that surprised me the most about the wedding was the fact that the bride did not get to enjoy the wedding. She plans everything but, then, is just on display all night long.

Another key thing to understand about Saudi Arabia is that many men and women have arranged marriages. The parents of the bride and groom select a mate for their children and find ways to introduce them. A wedding is one place were many mothers of sons are looking for their future daughter-in-law. A wedding has many single, eligible women all in one place, and mothers of sons are on the prowl, looking for their son's future wife. While it is not exactly the same as in the United States since we do not typically have arranged marriages, there is the idea that single people go to a wedding hoping to find their future mate. While there were many differences between the weddings I have been to in the United States compared to the wedding in Saudi Arabia, there are also plenty of similarities.

After a few days in Saudi Arabia, Leilah, her sister, and I traveled to Egypt. One of the first days we were there, Leilah talked to the concierge at the hotel and found out there was going to be a wedding at the hotel during our stay. She told them her friend from America is writing a book about weddings and would like to see an Egyptian wedding. The night of the wedding, Leilah and I got all dressed up and waited in the lobby in hopes to get a glimpse of the bride. Leilah's sister thought we were so silly for getting dressed up, but all three of us waited in the lobby for over an hour for the bride to arrive.

The hotel associates kept telling us the bride was coming down the stairs in the middle of the lobby, but she came a different way. I think they lied to us since we were a bit stalkerish. Before the bride arrived, the concierge walked us into the reception room, but we could only stay for a minute. Later, after the bride arrived, we snuck back in. We remained in the room, taking pictures and enjoying the festivities for about twenty minutes before we were caught and someone from the hotel told us we had to leave. One thing for sure, people know how to throw a wedding in the Middle East!

As the bride and groom entered, there was a whole production with belly dancers, drummers, musicians, and more. After the big, festive entrance, the bride and groom danced together. The room was fantastic; so many flowers and beautiful displays. The entry of the ballroom was a glowing floor pathway with tall vases and floating candles and, of course, a whole lot of flowers. There were even strands of fake flowers hanging from the ceiling the entire walkway. At the end of the walkway was a Cinderella carriage, pictures of the bride and groom, and a "wedding dress" made of white roses. The dance floor was the glowing floor and flowers hanging from the ceiling again. At the end of the bride and groom's first dance, there were fireworks all around the dance floor, confetti, and a fog machine. There were also two large projection screens so everyone in the large ballroom could see what was happening on the dance floor. It was a neat experience. I had never crashed a wedding before, and I could not believe how extravagant the wedding was.

Being able to experience weddings in a different culture is truly an experience of a lifetime. It opened my eyes to new things and understanding the similarities and differences between the various cultures. I am fortunate to have these experiences. If you ever get a chance to travel and crash a wedding, I would recommend it!

Lessons:

- Set a budget early in the planning process and stick to it as much as possible.
- The dollar amount you spend on your wedding should not matter as much as the guest list.
- Decide what traditions are important to you and your fiancé and be sure to incorporate them into the wedding day.
- If you get a chance, experience a wedding of another culture.

Notes:

Second Chances and Unexpected Weddings

Communication is the key to any relationship and the most important thing in a marriage. Keep the lines of communication open and never lie to your spouse. Always believe the best in your spouse and take their side no matter what.

Second Marriages

Everyone deserves to be cared for and loved. There are plenty of people in this world who choose to be single for one reason or another, but there are also many individuals who are out there looking for true love. Some people may be looking for their first love while others have been married before and have gotten divorced and looking for a second chance.

While everyone plans and hopes their marriage will last a lifetime, unfortunately, that is not always the case. Sometimes, things don't work out, and people get divorced. While I do not recommend this for anyone, I do understand there are lots of different reasons why people may get divorced. "About 40 to 50 percent of married couples in the United States divorce. The divorce rate for subsequent marriages is even higher" (American Psychological Association).

Marriage is hard work; something that you have to wake up every morning and choose to be married. You have to fight for your spouse and never take them for granted. As the years pass and people grow and change, sometimes, the couple stops communicating or putting their spouses needs first. Unfortunately, in our society, too many people think divorce is an easy out and stop trying to make their marriage work and choose to get divorced. Divorces are messy no matter who you are and are extremely painful for all parties involved. Even though someone has been divorced does not mean they do not deserve a second chance at true love. I have been to two weddings that were second marriages. I believe that everyone deserves to find happiness, and sometimes, that comes in second marriages.

Some people do not get as excited for a couple that is getting married for the second time, or they think they should have a smaller wedding. I believe this is up to the couple. Just because someone's first marriage did not work out does not mean they cannot throw a big wedding for their second marriage. People have a big wedding to celebrate their commitment and love for each other with their family and friends. Their passion and dedication for the second marriage are no less than that of their first. The first marriage just did not work out for one reason or another.

One part of the wedding planning process that would be different for a second marriage would be the registry. Typically, someone who is getting married for the second time would be a little bit older and already have many of the typical items that someone would put on their registry. The couple may decide to have a smaller registry or put unique items that they want on the registry. I have also heard of when a couple chooses to collect money for their favorite charity instead of gifts or money for themselves. They decided to give back to others and let their guests be a part of the giving spirit.

The two weddings I have been to that were second marriages both were very festive and fun. If you did not know these people were married before, you would have no idea this was their second wedding. Both weddings were unique and matched the couple's personality. I am glad I got to be a part of the special day for these couples.

The second marriages reminded me of the grace and love that God provides. I am a Christian who believes in God's love. I believe that he can restore all things and turn bad situations into good. While God does not want couples to get divorced, he provides grace and mercy and allows people to find love again. God is a loving God who wants the best for his people. I believe that everyone should be loved.

Unexpected Marriage

Along with second marriages, I have also been to a wedding that was unexpected. The couple was dating for a while and got pregnant out of wedlock. Getting pregnant was not something they had planned. They were young and figured they would get married eventually, but due to the pregnancy, they wanted to get married as soon as possible.

The couple's family and friends surrounded them with love and support, and we threw them a fabulous wedding. I worked closely with Alison and threw her a bridal shower and helped plan the whole day. Alison and Gerard are still happily married with two children. Getting pregnant out of wedlock may not have been what they were expecting or planned, but God has a way of turning things around and turning bad into good.

Till Death Do You Part

My advice is never let divorce be an option. Don't even put that on the table. Never threaten your spouse with divorce and don't go into a marriage thinking that if this does not work out, there is always divorce. I am a believer that if you are getting married, you are vowing to be with that person until death do you part. Cherish your spouse and work hard every day to keep the fire alive.

Coming from someone who is single and has never been married, I know that there is so much more to a marriage that I do not understand. It is one of those things that you don't know what you don't know. There is no rulebook or marriage manual to get you through the hard times. There will be hard times; life is messy and complicated, but you have to make a conscious effort to work on your marriage and love your spouse even when you hate them.

Communication is the key to any relationship and the most important thing in a marriage. Keep the lines of communication open and never lie to your spouse. Always believe the best in your spouse and take their side no matter what. Everyone needs someone in their corner, rooting for them. Be your spouse's biggest supporter and make sure they know that you love them. Random acts of kindness and love go a long way. Tell your spouse how you feel about them often; never just assume they know. People need to hear words of affirmation to be encouraged.

Love Languages

One great way to get to know your spouse and the best way to love them and be loved by them is to learn about your love languages. Everyone gives and receives love differently. There are five different love languages. The five love languages are the following: words of affirmation, quality time, receiving gifts, acts of service, and physical touch. Learn what you need to feel loved as well as what your partner needs.

Having a better understanding of yourself and what type of love language you need to feel loved as well as understanding what your spouse needs to feel loved will make a huge difference in your marriage for years to come. I would highly recommend reading the book *The 5 Love Languages: The Secret to Love that Lasts* by Gary Chapman. Reading this book as a couple is just one suggestion to help you build a healthy, long-lasting marriage or to make your second marriage last this time around.

Premarriage Counseling

I would also recommend that before you say, "I do," you go through some premarriage counseling. A good premarital counselor will be able to work with you and your fiancé to figure out some of the tough stuff before getting married, in hopes to prepare you for marriage better and ensure you set yourself up for a successful marriage.

I know one pastor who takes his job very seriously when it comes to officiating a wedding. He will not agree to marry any couple until they have sat down with him for a few sessions of premarital counseling. He also suggests that you do not pick your wedding date until you have completed your counseling sessions.

I know most couples do not do this, but it is certainly a good idea to begin counseling very early in the engagement process. The last thing you want to do is have a whole wedding planned and get so caught up in the excitement of the big day that you lose sight of the person you are marrying. Then, begin a few premarital counseling classes and realize your fiancé is not right for you, and you don't want to go through with the wedding. A good premarital counselor will be able to bring up any issues one partner might be hiding and work through any potential roadblocks that might come your way early in the marriage.

While I am a big proponent of premarital counseling, I am not naive and know that just because a couple goes through premarital counseling and works out their issues before getting married does not mean they are not going to have problems throughout their marriage. Marriage is difficult and takes love, patience, and communication. Unfortunately, throughout the years, one person or both just stops trying. They decide the marriage is no longer worth it and slowly become distant, and eventually, things end in divorce.

Lessons:

- Love is out there for all.
- Second marriages can still have a big wedding.
- God can turn any bad situation into good.
- Learn your love language.
- Take your vows seriously.
- Remember your vows when times get tough.
- Don't let divorce be an easy out.

Notes:

_____

_____

_____

_____

_____

_____

_____

_____

_____

_____

_____

_____

_____

_____

_____

_____

_____

_____

_____

_____

_____

_____

_____

_____

_____

_____

_____

_____

Thank-You Notes

Wedding favors are nice, but handwritten notes are more important.

Thank-You Cards Are a Must

Thank-you cards are a lost art these days. I have never been very good at sending thank-you notes but know that they are extremely important, and for things that matter most, I get them done. When it comes to your wedding, it is imperative that you write thank-you notes. Your guests took time out of their busy schedule to spend time with you to celebrate your wedding and spent money on a gift, so it is crucial that you tell them how much you appreciate them coming and the gift they bought you.

Sending thank-you cards also lets the guests know that you received their gifts. Many people will mail their gift or just drop it off at the gift table and not know if you ever got it. By sending a thank-you note, it provides confirmation that you received their gift, and you are showing them your appreciation.

Add a Personal Touch to the Thank-You Cards

One thing I loved that Jessica and Ryan did with their thank-you notes is they waited until they got their professional pictures back to send out their thank-you cards. They included a couple of pictures from the wedding in each thank-you card. This was a nice special touch with the thank-you notes. It is always nice to add a unique touch to your thank-you cards and personalize them. Depending on how big your wedding is, you will be writing a lot of thank-you cards, and it can become pretty cookie cutter.

The pictures add that personal touch, showing your guests that you went above and beyond and truly are thankful they attended your wedding, not to mention how appreciative you are for the gift they bought you. The pictures should be pictures of the guests you are sending the note to, not just pictures of you and your new spouse. While you might be excited about how great you look in your pictures, not everyone is going to want to display your photo around their house, unless they are in the picture too. You can try and get pictures with as many guests during the evening, but I also love those candid action shots on the dance floor pictures.

The thank-you note can be really simple, and most can be very similar, but if you can add a personalized detail for each note, that means a lot to the guests. The notes should be handwritten, never typed, and don't send an email. Emails are incredibly informal when it comes to this stuff; an actual handwritten note is necessary.

Start Writing the Thank-You Cards as You Receive the Gifts

With so many people buying their gifts online these days, it makes it easy to simply ship the gift directly to the couple before the wedding. You can even do this at most stores when you buy something from the registry. Being able to send the gift directly to the couple makes wedding gift shopping a breeze.

Not only does sending the gift directly to the couple make it easier on the guest, it also makes it easier on the couple. The day of the wedding, the guest does not have to worry about bringing the gift, and the couple does not have to worry about someone loading it up at the end of the night and transporting it home. Most people have to do at least some type of travel to weddings, so it is nice not to have to worry about lugging around a gift or forgetting it somewhere.

I am getting ready to head to Katelyn and Jim's wedding next weekend, and a couple of weeks ago, I got on Amazon, quickly ordered the couple's gift off their registry, had it shipped to their house directly, and had already received a thank-you card in the mail. I know Katelyn and Jim received the gift; they were able to show their appreciation, and it is one less thank-you card they have to worry about after the wedding. I, in turn, don't have to worry about traveling with the gift when I fly to the wedding.

You should send out thank-you cards within two weeks of receiving a wedding gift before the wedding and within a month after the wedding for all gifts you receive the week of or at the wedding. Sending thank-you cards in a timely manner is an imperative part of the thanking process. If you are planning on sending pictures or some other special touch with your thank you cards, you can wait to send all thank you cards until after the wedding. But I would recommend to at least write the note and wait to send it until you can add the special touch after the wedding.

Gift Table

Even though most people will mail you their gifts before or after the wedding, it is still a good idea to have a gift table and some container for cards. Some people will still bring a gift or card to the wedding and will need a place to put them. I would recommend some box or basket for the cards. It is too easy for a card to get lost, so have a specific container for the cards. I would recommend something that allows the guests to put the card in but not take them back out easily.

For guests, you should bring the gift to the reception and not the ceremony. Unless everything is all in one location, your gift is likely to get lost in the shuffle, is cumbersome, and there will be nowhere to put it at the ceremony. Keep your gift in the car until you get to the reception.

It is also a good idea for the couple to assign someone before the wedding to take care of transporting all the gifts from the reception to their house after the wedding. Many times, this might be the bridesmaids or family members, but if you have someone assigned early, then, this is one less thing to think about during the wedding day.

Wedding Registries

Wedding registries are extremely helpful for both the guests and the couple. Without a registry, you will get a bunch of junk that you don't want. I am sure you will still get a bunch of things you don't want with a registry, but it limits that significantly. There is always that one friend or crazy aunt who thinks they know what you like and refuses to buy something off the registry. If you are going to get gifts, you might as well get things you actually want. Register at a few different stores to provide variety and ease for your guests. Put more items on your registry than you think you should have with varying price levels so all guests can find something they would like to purchase. You can also let your guests know you would like cash for something specific like your honeymoon or down payment on a house.

One caveat with the whole cash suggestion is to keep in mind a specific use for it. People want to be giving money to a particular cause or fund. So if you really want more cash than gifts, make sure you indicate what you want to use the money for in your invitation. As an attendee, giving cash is sometimes the easiest option, and let's be honest who doesn't like cash?

Although, I have heard horror stories of people stealing the envelopes of cash right off the gift table at weddings. Like I mentioned before, I would suggest providing a box or something that guests can slip their card with money into but can't get their hands in to take anything out. While I always like to think the best of people and can't imagine someone doing this, but desperate times comes extreme actions, and it is a lot easier to steal a card full of cash than a big gift. This is just something to keep in mind when you are thinking about your gift table. This is certainly not something that happens regularly, but it has happened, so it is good to be aware.

Think long term, not just now when making your registry. I have talked to some of my friends who have been married for a few years now, and they said they wished they registered for more practical items and less "fun, one-time-use items." It sounds great to have a margarita machine now, but five years and two kids later, you are not using that machine anymore.

Mike and Melissa had a hard time with their registry because they did not like the concept of people buying them gifts. While they understood that people would purchase them gifts for their wedding, they did not want to make a registry. For every item over one hundred dollars Melissa would put on the registry, Mike would put something less than fifty dollars to try and balance it out.

I have also heard of couples that genuinely did not want their guests to buy anything for them, so they set up a fund for a charity and asked their guests to donate to this charity in their name instead of buying gifts. This is certainly something honorable, and each couple can do whatever they wish for their big day. Now, I don't know about you, but one of the best parts of having a wedding is all the fun gifts people buy you. Most people understand that when you are invited to a wedding, you will then be expected to fork out some cash to buy a gift.

Let me tell you; I am someone who is oh so very familiar with this concept. For all the weddings I have been to and all the gifts I have purchased for others, I fully expect my friends to do the same for me. One of the things I have noticed though over the years as I have gotten older and attended weddings of friends who are a few years out of college and more established, their wedding registries certainly reflected the maturity and need for more expensive and practical items. Waiting until you are older to get married does have some perks. Your friends are more established and can buy you nicer things.

Wedding Favors

Another aspect that goes along with thanking your guests is the idea of providing them with a wedding favor the night of the wedding. People either set these at each place setting on the tables or they set them out toward the end of the wedding for people to grab on their way out. I have seen favors such as wine stoppers, small plants, seeds to grow a plant, homemade marmalade, local snacks, homemade doughnuts, and more.

At Nick and Tara's wedding, a candy bar was set up toward the end of the night for guests to grab a bag and fill it with all sorts of candy as their favor. This is a simple and relatively cheap favor you can do for your guests, but many people are not interested in a whole bag of candy, and the bride and groom typically end up with a lot of leftover candy.

One favor I saw that I liked was a mason jar filled with Hershey's Kisses. The mason jar and tag on the jar matched the theme of the wedding, and the jars were set out at each place setting. The Hershey's Kisses provided a little treat at the wedding, and mason jars can always come in handy. This was certainly one of the more practical favors I have seen. It is also relatively easy to do and on the cheaper side which certainly helps with the budget and time constraints when preparing for the wedding.

One other thing I have seen in lieu of wedding favors for the guests was the couple donated to their favorite charity in honor of their guests. This is certainly something I find most practical and good use of your money. While I understand the concept of providing wedding favors to your guests and how it is a tradition, but in my opinion, no one really needs this junk, and it is a waste of money.

Wedding favors are nice, but handwritten notes are more important. I have thrown away just about all the wedding favors I have ever gotten. You are trying to buy a gift for all of your attendees, and that can get pricey. Save the money and upgrade your bar or food options before spending money on junk that people don't need. Or as I mentioned before, using that money to get pictures developed and add a photo or two of each guest at the wedding in the thank-you note.

Some people may disagree with me on this concept, as it is tradition to give your guests a favor, but I just don't see the point. Unless you want to spend a lot of time making something personal and or a lot of money on something you think all your guests will really want, it is just not worth it, in my opinion. At the end of the night, when most of your guests are drunk and walking back to their hotel room, what they really need is a late-night snack, not a cheap trinket they will throw away. Spend the money on late-night wings or pizza or other greasy food many of your guests will enjoy. You can work this out with your caterer to be set out the last hour of the reception for your guests to enjoy a "late-night pick-me-up" at the end of the evening. Your guests will thank you for the late-night snack and won't think twice about not having a wedding favor.

Lessons:

- Thank-you notes are not old school and should be sent.
- Never send a wedding thank-you via email.
- A gift registry is critical if you want to receive gifts you actually want.
- Create your registry with your fiancé.
- Put more items on your registry than you think at varying price levels.
- Register early.
- Don't spend a whole lot of time or money on wedding favors.

Notes:

_____

Happily Ever After

Your wedding day will come and go, but the person standing beside you should be there for a lifetime. Strive to be the person they fell in love with every single day.

Goal of Marriage

The goal of marriage is to find someone to do life with, love, and cherish till death do you part. If you can find this and be happy, then, you are incredibly lucky. One of my favorite couples in my life, Mr. Richard and Ms. Janice, just celebrated their sixtieth wedding anniversary. They met when they were in kindergarten and have spent a lifetime together. Richard and Janice are the cutest couple, raised two kids, and figured out the secret of living a happy life together. Although, they will be the first to tell you that it was not always an easy road, but through it all, they have always loved each other.

Richard and Janice are the most generous people I know and are always looking to help someone in need. They have lived a beautiful life together and still enjoy each other's company. They have both worked hard throughout their lives and are still busy as can be at eighty years old, constantly doing things for others. They have their routines and favorite restaurants for meals, but the love and respect that they show each other is contagious. I have enjoyed many meals with Richard and Janice, and while they may not know it, I have taken notes on how they live their life and strive to have a marriage like theirs one day.

One of my favorite stories from Richard and Janice is when Richard decided to redo Janice's bathroom. Richard and Janice have always had separate bathrooms in their house. I think this may be one of the secrets to them staying together for so long. Anyway, Richard wanted to put in a new shower for Janice in her bathroom, and Janice agreed this would be a good idea. Little did Janice know this was going to be a much bigger production than she anticipated. Richard is a very handy man with multiple workshops and every tool you could imagine, so he was planning on doing the work himself as per usual.

"Honey, I am just about done installing your new shower. Do you want to come look?" Richard yelled downstairs.

Janice walked upstairs to see her new bathroom, and what does she see? A complete mess. "Richard, you are not almost done, it is a mess in here. Where is my toilet? And what about my sink?" Janice exclaimed.

"Oh, don't worry, honey, I am going to replace those too," Richard replied.

"It has already been three weeks. I don't think I can take much more of this," Janice said.

"It won't take much longer. I promise," Richard replied.

"Richard, we have had a wonderful life together, and one of the things that has helped keep our marriage lasting so many years is our two separate bathrooms," Janice argued back.

"Janice, I know, I know, sharing a bathroom with me has been harder than you thought," Richard said.

"Harder than I expected, that is an understatement! I feel like I am living in an African hut," Janice exclaimed.

"Whoa, whoa, whoa, now, you are exaggerating a bit. It is not that hard to share a bathroom with me," Richard replied.

"Not that hard! The bathroom always smells, you don't put the toilet seat down, and your shave clippings are always in the sink. There is no place for me to hang my towels or do my makeup. I do my makeup in my closet without a mirror. I have had enough!" Janice explained.

"Wow, okay, I understand, honey. I will call our nephew, Brian, right now and see if he can come over tomorrow to help me finish up the bathroom so that you can have your space back," said Richard.

"Thank you, dear! You know that having my own bathroom is what helps make this marriage work. If you want to keep it that way, you will finish the bathroom tomorrow," Janice said jokingly.

"I better sleep with one eye open tonight," Richard said, chuckling.

Work on Your Marriage Every Day

Being married is not easy. You have to wake up every day and choose to be married. You have to work on your marriage every day and make a choice to love your spouse. Marriage is about sacrifice, compromise, and putting your spouse's needs in front of your own. When you get married, you make this vow, and you need to choose to live by it every day to have a happy, lifelong marriage. Troubles and temptations will come your way, but you have to decide to be stronger than it. Life can throw curve balls at you left and right, and you need a partner to stand strong with you no matter what.

Some advice I have heard from happily married couples are to put each other first; never go to bed angry; when all else fails, take off your clothes, and after the sex, talk through whatever issues you had before the sex, and most likely, you will be able to find a compromise.

I cannot speak from personal experience since I am not married, but I have been around enough married couples to know that the excitement and love that you feel in the beginning takes a lot of work to keep the flame going years down the road. Too often in our society, couples take the easy way out and get a divorce instead of working on their problems. Years go by, and they stop listening and communicating with each other. Their kids grow up and leave home or their sense of self changes due to changes at work or home. Then, all of a sudden ten years pass, and they don't know how they got to this point. This stage where they believe there is no coming back.

Don't let yourself ever get to that point. Take your vows seriously. Commit every day to your spouse and don't ever take them for granted. Remember that your wedding day is only one day, but your marriage should last a lifetime. Don't get too caught up in the stress of planning the wedding. Don't let the planning process cause fights with your fiancé. Enjoy the process and spend more time falling in love with the person you want to spend the rest of your life with than the details of one day.

Don't Jump too Quickly or Settle for the Wrong Man

Be cautious not to jump into marriage too quickly. The early stages of a relationship are always fun and exciting. You think you love this person and feel the pressure to move quickly. Maybe, you feel the pressure from friends or family to get married and start a family. Maybe, being married or being a mom is your heart's desire, and you will do whatever it takes to get there. I urge you to take the time to get to know your partner before walking down the aisle. The last thing you want to do is marry the wrong person for the wrong reasons.

Don't ever feel trapped or stuck in a relationship or engagement. While it is not easy, breaking off an engagement is a whole lot simpler and less painful than being in a terrible marriage and getting divorced later down the road or staying in an unhealthy marriage.

I had a courageous, strong friend, Amelia, who broke off her engagement. Breaking off her engagement was probably the hardest decision she ever had to make. Amelia loved and cared for her fiancé but just had this gut feeling as things were getting serious with the wedding planning that something was not right. She had dreamt of her wedding day, and the guy she was going to marry, and things were not lining up. Amelia was very torn for a long time, trying to figure out what to do. She was not sure if it was just nerves of taking a big step and committing to someone or a genuine gut feeling of something was not right.

In the end, she knew what she needed to do and was so courageous and broke off the engagement. This was no easy task and honestly took a couple of years for her to get over but, now, she is in such a better place. Amelia was so glad she did what she knew she had to do. Too often, women get so caught up in wanting to be loved and cherished that they will settle for the wrong man even when they know it is not right.

Luckily for Amelia, she knew what she needed to do and took action. She was heartbroken, and it took years, but now, she is happily married to the man of her dreams. She found the true love of her life—a man who respects her, treats her well, and wants to spend the rest of his life loving and caring for her. Don't ever settle; your prince charming is out there!

Hannah's Three Rules of Dating

I have a few basic rules when it comes to dating in hopes to find the right guy for me. I believe you have to be open-minded and give people a chance. Dating is hard for both men and women, so you have to give people a chance. I will go out on a date with just about anyone once—within reason, of course. If things go reasonably well, I will go on a second date. First dates can be awkward, so as long as I was able to hold a decent conversation, we have things in common, and the guy was not a total crazy person, I will go out on date number two. Depending on how date number two goes will determine if I want to pursue things further or politely send them on their way.

My second rule is the red-rose test. I love red roses. I know, I know, it is cliché, but I can't help it, I love red roses. I make sure I bring this up in conversation, sometimes casually but most of the times directly. If I don't get red roses from the guy within the first three months of dating, then, I know I need to end the relationship. The first few months are the most exciting and passionate months. You want to spend all your time with the other person, get to know them as much as you can, and do special things for them to make sure they know you care. If a guy I am dating does not pick up on the fact that I love red roses and does not buy me them within the first three months, then, I am never going to get red roses from him.

Most guys love the chase and will do whatever it takes to get you early on in the relationship. If they are not picking up on things that you like and doing special things for you early, then, they will never do them later on. This brings me to rule number three. Never change for someone and don't expect to change someone else. I have a saying when I am on a first date, "This is what you get, I am who I am." Don't ever try to conform to what you think a guy wants you to be and don't enter into a relationship thinking you can change someone. You have to like the person for who they are, not who you think they can be or who you want them to be.

Don't ever settle. You deserve the best and are worthy to be loved and cherished by someone who will stand beside you and fight for you every day of your lives. It is never too late to back out of an engagement, but I would suggest you do it before you spend all the time and money planning the wedding. But if you need to run and leave someone at the altar, that is better than a life of unhappiness.

While it is typical to have cold feet or some nervousness about your wedding day and the person you are marrying, it is not okay to be terrified or have the uneasy gut feeling like you are doing the wrong thing. Listen to both your gut and your heart and do what is best for you. Hopefully, you are at the point where you are honestly in love and so excited to plan your perfect day with your future spouse.

Your wedding day will come and go, but the person standing beside you should be there for a lifetime. Strive to be the person they fell in love with every single day. While the wedding day is fun and exciting to plan, keep your heart focused on the person you are marrying and not just the excitement of the big day. Your wedding day will be fantastic no matter what happens, as long as you are marrying your best friend. If at the end of the day you are married, then, it will be a good day. Keep your eye on the prize and don't sweat the small stuff.

Lessons:

- The wedding is just one day; your marriage is the rest of your life.
- Fall in love with your spouse every day.
- Marriage is hard and requires work.
- Make sure you are marrying the right person for you, don't ever settle.

Notes:

REFERENCES

10 Registry Tips That'll Make Your Wedding Gifts So Much Better. Theknot. com. www.theknot.com/content/tips-on-registering-for-wedding-gifts.

2017. *The Wedding Processional Order: Who Walks When? Bridal Guide.* www.bridalguide.com/planning/wedding-ceremony-traditions/the-wedding-processional-order.

American Psychological Association. www.apa.org/topics/divorce/.

Band vs DJ: Which Is Best for You. Wedding Planning, Planning a Wedding, How to Plan a Wedding. www.perfectweddingguide.com/wedding-ideas/wedding-music-songs/band-vs-dj-which-is-best-for-you/.

Bindley, Katherine. 2011. *Wedding Etiquette: The Do's and Don'ts of Being a Guest. The Huffington Post.* www.huffingtonpost.com/2011/06/17/wedding-etiquette-the-dos_n_879354.html.

Glantz, Jen. 2017. *When to Ask Bridesmaids to Be in Wedding. Brides.* www.brides.com/story/when-to-ask-bridesmaids-to-be-in-wedding.

Lord, Maggie. 2013. *Things to Consider Before Booking Your Wedding Venue.* https://www.huffingtonpost.com/maggie-lord/things-to-consider-before_b_2951830.html.

Outdoor Wedding? Yes, You Need a Backup Plan. www.theknot.com/content/outdoor-wedding-backup-plan.

Save-the-Date Etiquette. www.theknot.com/content/save-the-dates-etiquette.

Steinberg, Stephanie. 2011. *How Much Does It Cost to Be a Bridesmaid?* CNN, Cable News Network. www.cnn.com/2011/LIVING/06/28/bridesmaids.cost/index.html.

Wedding Budget 101. www.theknot.com/content/wedding-budget-ways-to-save-money.

Wedding Traditions: Meaning of "Something Old, Something New...?" www.theknot.com/content/wedding-traditions-the-meaning-of-something-old.

Zaleski, Jessica. 2017. *Top Tips to Choosing Your Wedding Party.* www.theknot.com/content/tips-for-who-to-pick-as-bridesmaids.

ABOUT THE AUTHOR

Hannah grew up in rural Pennsylvania, and after high school, she attended Towson University in Maryland. She has a bachelor's degree in elementary/special education and taught special education for two years in Baltimore County before deciding it was not the right career fit for her.

After working a few different jobs, Hannah went back to school and received her master's in business administration from the University of Baltimore. Throughout her time in graduate school, she decided to do a career change and transition into the hospitality industry. She spent time working at the Baltimore Marriott Inner Harbor at Camden Yards in Maryland and the Charleston Marriott in South Carolina, in both the banquet and event management departments. Hannah has worked countless weddings on both the planning and operations teams, ensuring that the day of the wedding runs flawlessly. She has seen the good, the bad, and the ugly when it comes to weddings and believes that she has seen enough to know the ins and outs of how to plan the perfect wedding.

In her free time, Hannah enjoys going to the beach, kayaking, and paddle boarding. She also enjoys watching movies and ballroom dancing with her boyfriend.

CPSIA information can be obtained
at www.ICGtesting.com
Printed in the USA
LVHW041201171120
671900LV00006B/458